i

## Volume Two

## Ballycurragh to Tasmania 1649 – 1868
## The Grey Family and Innes Clan Volume Two

# Ballycurragh to Tasmania 1649 – 1868
# The Grey Family and Innes Clan Volume Two

Encompassing 'A STORY OF A PIONEER FAMILY in Van Diemen's Land'
By Kate Hamilton Dougharty (2018 Edition)

Written and edited by Ian Broinowski

Illustrated by Richard Chuck

Contributions by Paddy Murray and Paddy Heaney (Ireland)

Jim Everett-puralia meenamatta

ISBN - 978-0-9923735-5-9

# Dedication

*This book is dedicated to*
*Paddy Murray and his beloved Roscomroe*
*01/05/1939 - 30/07/2018*

# Contents

# PART THREE: FILLING IN THE BOXES

# Introduction to Part Three: Filling in the Boxes

Written by Dr Ian Broinowski

Foraging is a primeval drive for historians. It is in their DNA and leads to a lifetime of digging through dusty archives, old tobacco tins, torn photos, decaying cemeteries, shoe boxes, crusty suitcases and anything which may give them a lead, a window to the magic of the past. They turn things over, study, discard, classify, reclaim until their jigsaw begins to take shape. Usually with more gaps than fill but enough to be tantalizing. Sometimes others look again at their puzzle of fragments and reinterpret it themselves. History is a never-ending search, evolving and redressing. Below are boxes full of fragments from my research into the family and the events which influenced their life. They are by their very nature incomplete, waiting for time to reveal more but enough for you to gain just a little more insight into Katie's story.

It is unsurprising that Kate Dougharty lived in the imaginary world of her ancestors and loved ones. The latter years of her life she spent in St Luke's Hospital in Launceston suffering from debilitating arthritis and experiencing long lonely nights particularly through the winters of Tasmania. Surrounded by musty old letters, pictures, personal diaries and a head filled with stories from her grandmother, Lysbeth, great aunts Henrietta and Catherine, she began to create miniature vignettes of lives past and almost overlooked. We are the beneficiaries of her stories and fantasies.

Reading her book I found myself feeling uneasy. It was neither strictly a history book, nor fiction and at times seemed to lead into uncountable directions. Eventually I began to realise that it is more akin to theatre; it evokes the life and atmosphere of the stage. We are taken into a myriad of colorful scenes with real people whose lives passed nearly two centuries ago. They cover confronting times; decisions to emigrate, shipwreck, building their homes, schools, marriages and of course terrible tragedies.

The beauty is in the minute detail of her descriptions of the dresses, laying the dinner table, parties and most of all her unequivocal woman's perspective. She saw the world through her female relative's eyes. They were Protestant, Irish, independently spirited and reasonably wealthy. Her writing unashamedly reflects this and while it may now seem dated and at times a little perplexing it does provide us with a unique window into the lives of the small isolated community of Avoca in the very early years of European settlement in Van Diemen's Land.

Editing however proved challenging. Initially it was my intention to keep Kates' work intact, with footnotes to provide background information and corrections. While this was a noble goal it proved to be less achievable in practice. There were some specific issues with the original text which were difficult to overcome. Katie learned her writing skills, grammar and punctuation growing up in the late 1800s. Writing styles have changed and evolved since that period especially in the use of commas, which for current readers makes it slower and distracting.

There were also some factual errors, which is quite understandable given that Katie was bed ridden and had limited access to archival material. (She would have loved the internet!) For example she cited Lt James Gray as being unmarried when infact he arrived with his wife Mary, a young child and another born three weeks after their arrival. Katie also mixed up the place in the family of Lysbeth and Henrietta. She had the former as the youngest while infact it was the reverse. Humphrey Grey was given the rank of Major in the book but no substantiating evidence can be found to support this. Generally military rank could be applied for life but on no occasions does Humphrey use this title. However I am open to being proven wrong on this. Footnotes for such corrections seemed cumbersome and annoying for the reader so the obvious errors have been simply been altered in the text. Each scene described by Katie has more to it than the audience can see before them. 'Filling in the Boxes' takes you behind the scenes of each chapter and offers a little extra material to think about.

Finally, like Katie and most other historical researchers I will probably have made mistakes too. It is the nature of the beast so if you find any errors please let us know and we can make the alteration in any further editions.


Ian Broinowski

# BOX ONE: EXPEDITION INTO IRELAND, LT COLONEL JOHN GRAY

## Expedition into Ireland Lt. Colonel John Gray[xx]

Lieutenant Colonel John Gray was born into challenging and dangerous times. England was in conflict with itself, a violent, destructive civil war lasting from 1642 – 1651 the ramifications of which lasted for centuries, and was especially poignant for Ireland. Gray, like all his kinsfolk, had to choose: Parliament or King. There was nothing in between and once decided, so too was not only his own fate but also the destiny of his family and future generations. With Gray's family background and a religious persuasion likely to have been Presbyterian, he chose for Parliament and Cromwell which led to a life of military activity and war for many years to come. He was certainly an active participant in some of the most significant battles both on English soil and especially in bloody and violent conflicts in Ireland.

### Military Life

The first extant reference to Gray is on the 28 April 1645 with the list of Officers to serve under Colonel Gray in Lincolnshire.

¶Ordered, That it be referred to the Committee of both Kingdoms, to grant Commissions to these Officers, under the Command of Colonel Henry Gray, in Lyncolnshire: Lieutenant Colonel Wm. Chandler, Captain Peter Stubber Major, Captain Andrew Ruddocke Nath. Wright, Lieutenant James Kingsborow Ensign to Captain Ruddocke, Rob't Russell Captain Lieutenant John Gray Ensign to the Colonel.[xxi]

Perhaps the most revealing aspect of this first record is the location and list of names. While no definitive records have been located which place Gray in Lincolnshire, some speculation is justified. The period in question is complex. Traditionally armies had been formed from local districts under the command of aristocratic families and rank offered through favours. The major problem with this arrangement for Parliament was the fierce loyalty the soldiers had to their own families, property and lands which meant they were often reluctant to leave their homes undefended and vulnerable to attack.

This happened to the 2nd Earl of Stamford, Henry Grey, whose Bradgate House was attacked in 1642 by Prince Rupert and his family's arch rival and neighbour Colonel Hastings, Catholic and Royalist, 'whence they took all his arms, and took away and spoiled all his goods and certainly with the intention of killing his children.'[xxii] The situation is confusing. In February 1645 Parliament had established the New Model Army centrally controlled and independent of local loyalties. Clearly it would have taken time to implement while there remained some armies operating independently during this time.

The question arises whether Gray had been recruited in April/May from Lincolnshire or further afield. Henry Grey's estates were in neighbouring Leicester and

Rutland. The other factor is that Gray, as a junior officer, an ensign, had been assigned to the Colonel, Henry Grey. Whether this is a coincidence or there was some family connection is unknown although the latter would seem to be a more likely scenario, a notion supported by Evans (1995) who stated that 'Stamford could and did exert personnel preferences in his choice of officers' when referring to the appointment of Captain Edward Gray.[xxiii]

The family lore that John Gray was Scottish seems unlikely although his family may well have come from there originally, or at least had close connections. At this time, Scotland had their own army which remained independent and generally accepted only their own. Gray appears from this to have been English and would more likely have joined the army in his local area. To date no further family connection to the Gray line has been identified although his later marriage to the Presbyterian Basil family with its aristocratic pedigree and connection would certainly indicate that Gray's family was eligible for such a union to occur.

It may also have been that Gray was a younger son whose destiny, by English tradition, would naturally lead to a career in the Military or Church, leaving the eldest to inherit whatever estates or property the family may have had. However, it is worth taking time to view his situation in the context of the values, ideals and ambitions of the men and families he was now associated with.

Two important players in the political and military events of the time were the 2nd Earl of Stamford, Henry Gray and his son, Thomas, known as Lord Gray of Groby. Thomas played significant roles in the dramatic events of the times as had their families for centuries.[xxiv] The Grays of Bradgate Park were a high-born aristocratic family, believed by many to have descended from Anchitell De Grey, who was part of the Norman invasion of William the Conqueror in 1066 and who was suitably rewarded.[xxv]

Their subsequent history is, to say the least, turbulent and eventful. Their fortunes soared when, in 1464, Elizabeth Grey (Woodville) married King Edward IV, a Yorkist, after the death of her husband, Sir John Grey, in the War of the Roses.

The family fell under Edward's brother, Richard III who had Elizabeth's children killed in the Tower. Known ever since as, 'The Princes in the Tower' they were believed to have been murdered because they posed a risk to Richard's claim to the throne. Later the Gray family returned their allegiances to the Lancastrians and the Tudors, and after the Battle of Bosworth Field in 1485, they were well established and an integral part of Henry Tudor's court. Their estate, Bradgate Park, was soon to be built by the second Marquis of Dorset as a hunting lodge during the late 1400's.

Intrigue and politics were never far away from the family, who played for high stakes indeed through marriage and disposable assets such as daughters. As a result, Lady Jane Grey was Queen of England for just nine days in 1554 before Mary Tudor, Henry VIII's daughter, took power in the most decisive way. Her title, 'Bloody Mary', was well deserved. It is interesting to note that the family who benefited most from these events was of course the Hasting family; a feud between the two families simmered for generations, only to surface once again in the Civil War.

The failed attempt at gaining the Crown had a devastating effect on Grey power, wealth and lands. It was not until the 1600s and the Stuarts, James I and ironically Charles I that the family's fortunes began to improve. This enabled them to 'purchase one of the baronetcies sold to fund the plantations of Ulster' and gain titles of Lord Grey of Groby in 1603 and in 1628, The Earl of Stamford.[xxvi] By the 1640s, Henry Grey was the Earl of Stamford and his son Thomas, Lord Grey of Groby.

Wars are terrible but perhaps civil wars are the worst of all. Here we have a family divided in matters of life and death. Henry, the father, is a supporter of Parliament, but also a moderate Presbyterian, and while he clearly wanted Charles I removed, he did not support his execution. His son, Thomas, on the other hand, became more and more entrenched with Cromwell and his radical elite. He was well regarded and successful as a military commander even in his late teens, and over time increased his fame, power and fortune until he inevitably became a threat to Cromwell. He was one of the Commissioners at the trial of Charles I and second signature on the Death Warrant of the King, above that of Oliver Cromwell. Thomas, in his mid 20s, was one of only two nobles who signed the document. Perhaps it was by good fortune he died of gout aged 34 before the restoration of Charles II. Had he not, his fate would most certainly have been settled in a way befitting the times.

The rift between father and son became bitter and acrimonious, culminating when Thomas returned from the trial and was asked by his father, 'King or no King', he replied, 'No King my Lord', at which point Henry responded, 'Then no Lord Grey!' and left in disgust.[xxvii] To add to the mix, Thomas' younger brother, Anchitel Grey, fought for the Royalists!

John Gray, as a young ensign, was most certainly associated with this family in some way. His selection and assignment to the Colonel could have led him into the sphere of turbulent power play and spasmodic military action. However, by this time, Stamford's military engagements came to an end with the defeat at the Battle of Ledbury. While he had been a keen supporter of Parliament for the previous few years, his military and leadership skills were sorely lacking, not surprising considering his only experience had been as a rather cantankerous, authoritarian lord of the manor.

Over time he became a less enchanted with Cromwell's thirst for power and control. His move to quiet retirement may have paved the way for his pardon after the Restoration and regaining his estates and of course, having at least one son on the side of royalty may have helped!

So where did this leave John Gray?

It was a time well suited to ambitious, talented men who were encouraged and rewarded for their successes. The New Model Army under Cromwell promoted men for their ability rather than social standing, which clearly accentuated the difference between the two sides. Gray was in an ideal position to move up the ranks and gain from this process both in status and materially. It also seems that he was now closely associated with soon-to-become Colonel Peter Stubber. The next glimpse of Gray is in Ireland in April 1648 and his adventures with the infamous Lord Inchiquin.

> In accordance with the order of the House of Commons of 13th April last, Beck, the auditor, is to audit and state the accounts for Irish service of Col. Sir A. Loftus, Lieut.-Col. Geo. Hooper, Captains W. Fynte, Thos. Hart, John Jefford, Henry Gibbon, Capt.-Lieut. Dudley Loftus, Lieuts. Adam Loftus and Edward Westby, marshal. officers of Sir A. Loftus' regiment; also of Col. Stubber (Col. of a regiment of foot in Munster), John Gray, Major of that regiment, Thomas Davies, lieutenant in it, and of Capt. Alex. Barrington, capt. of a company of Col. Needham's regiment. These officers are come over and were driven from their commands under Lord Inchiquin.

The following minutes are from the 11 May 1648

1648.

> (3)  To the following officers of Col. Stubber's regiment :—
> Col. Stubber, Major John Gray, Capts. Thomas Chandler, Samuel Playford, Andrew Ruddock, Lieuts. Thomas Davies, Bennyworth, and Wm. Battle, to Ensign John Gething, and Qr.-Mr. Wm. Stotesbury.

xxix

The first thing to notice here is that Gray is now a Major. The fact that he seems to have been associated with the foot regiments may have helped. The horse or cavaliers were generally higher in prestige and status, coveted by the aristocracy, which made advancement far more difficult. Even though Cromwell's aim was to promote through merit clearly the entrenched English class system was not so easily obliterated. The foot regiments on the other hand provided opportunities for promotion far more readily for men such as Stubber and Gray who may well have found such a setting suited their personal desires and quests for power and riches.

It would seem from the above that both men had been sent to Ireland sometime after 1646 to assist a gentleman by the name of Murrough O'Brien, 1st Earl of Inchiquin, (1614-74) whose ancestors dated back to the early kings of Ireland. He and his family were Protestant. Real life, it is said, is far more intriguing than fiction and if Inchiquin's story had been created by the mind of an author, it is doubtful whether it would ever have been believed!

As a young man, Inchiquin fought with the Spanish Army in Italy in 1638 – 40 and returned to become the Vice President of Muster (southern Ireland). At first he fought for Charles I, but when he was snubbed by the King at Oxford and his ambition to become the President of Muster was thwarted, he switched sides to Parliament in July 1644. He promptly expelled all Catholics from Cork, Youghal and Kinsale and was duly awarded the Presidency of Munster by Parliament.

Gray and Stubber served with Inchiquin during 1647 and part of 1648. His regiments were involved with the storm of the Rock of Cashel in September, Battle of Knocknanuss, in November and the taking of Carrick on Suir in February 1648. He and his army had a terrible reputation during this period, as shown by the following quote from the British Civil Wars, Commonwealth & Protectorate 1638 – 1660;

Inchiquin decided to assert his authority in Munster by mounting a military offensive against the Confederates during the summer and autumn of 1647. He stormed and captured Dungarvin, Cappoquin and other garrisons gaining a terrible reputation amongst the Irish as *Murchadh na d'Tóiteán* "Murrough the Burner", after his troops stormed the Rock of Cashel, where they burned down the defences, massacred soldiers, civilians and priests and desecrated the Cathedral of St Patrick.[xxx]

Gray was clearly by now a well-seasoned and blooded soldier. The fact that he had been promoted showed he was well respected, although there was, naturally, a high mortality rate in his chosen profession. At this time, a familiar narrative begins to play out. Inchiquin was far from London, and Ireland at that time was not a priority for Parliament and he felt he received scant support or recognition for his efforts. Like Henry Gray, he too became increasingly alarmed at the actions and intent of the small but very powerful Parliamentary radicals who were now taking control. So, after years of slaughtering and exiling his fellow Irishmen and women he once again switched sides and declared for the King in April 1648.

Hence Gray and those who remained loyal to Parliament were forced to hastily leave and return to England. It seems doubtful that Gray would have any such qualms or quavering allegiances. Now Gray and Stubber are in England by the middle of 1648 with a rather uncertain future, although the war still provided each with employment and opportunities.

Kind Charles I of England, Scotland and Ireland was executed on the 30 January 1649. This event affected almost everyone, including John Gray. His friend and military compatriot, Peter Stubber, was in the King's Guard of Halberdiers at the time of his death. While no one is certain who his executioner was, it seems very likely that it was Stubber who ended the Reign and life of a King.[xxxi] The Commonwealth Parliament and Ireland

Greater political and military events once again dictated Gray's direction in life. The killing of a king does not end a war. In fact, it only intensified with Charles II being King of Scotland, plotting from France and naturally with an eye to Ireland as an obvious place to launch an attack on England to restore the monarchy. Certainly that was in line with Cromwell's thinking at this time. He needed to quell Ireland, quickly and decisively, and so began the Irish campaign of 1649.

Needless to say, England was in financial and economic crisis: added to this the country experienced a serious famine in the same year: harvests and crops failed, leaving no room for further taxes and fund raising. Armies, especially a permanent one, cost dearly and soldiers were without pay for months at a time. Cromwell solved the problem with the simple promise of Irish land in return for service. There was however problems with this notion: generally, land was occupied and the owners were somewhat reluctant to leave. Cromwell settled this matter unswervingly through genocide, enforced slavery and the Plantation (settlement) of Protestant English in their place. A primary mantra for any war is to first demonise your enemy and as Paddy Murray (unpublished) pointed out he and his soldiers arrived with well entrenched views of their enemy;

In 1646, English man Sir John Temple, in his book wrote an exaggerated account of the massacres, as factual of the Irish uprising five years earlier in 1641, there was a certain element of truth to his allegation, though nothing on the scale suggested, it did inflame anti-Catholic and Irish feeling. Cromwell perhaps Grey arrived in Ireland believing the Irish to be barbarous and bloodthirsty.

Cromwell landed at Ringsend, Dublin on the 15th August 1649 with 12,000 troops, including Colonel Peter Stubber with his own regiment of foot soldiers. While there is no direct evidence that Gray was with him at this time, it seems a reasonable assumption that he was, as Stubber was still writing to Parliament as late as 1657 in order to secure land and payment for Gray.

Stubber's regiment was raised in May 1649 from a group of disbanded volunteers in Kent, many of whom were captured Royalists. Their reputation was atrocious, and they were well known as plunderers and worse. They marched to Chester 'in a disorderly fashion' and in June to the West Country, where their nickname of 'Gorum's Bastards' was well deserved for their thievery.[xxxii]

Later that year they landed at Dublin and in September fought with Cromwell at Drogheda, on the River Boyne. The grotesque events of this battle are well documented and make for grim and confronting reading. Suffice to say, Gray was involved with one of the most infamous events in Irish history leaving thousands dead, all apparently at the behest of Cromwell's (Protestant) God and in his words;

"I am persuaded that this is a righteous judgment of God upon these barbarous wretches, who have imbued their hands in so much innocent blood and that it will tend to prevent the effusion [shedding] of blood for the future, which are satisfactory grounds for such actions, which otherwise cannot but work remorse and regret." (Letter to Speaker 17 September 1649 Oliver Cromwell after the storming of Drogheda)[xxxiii]

Gray was certainly present at this event and is listed as one of 'The soldiers of the Commonwealth" (1649) who were were making claims on the Commonwealth for their military service with Cromwell[xxxiv]

**SOLDIERS OF THE COMMONWEALTH. 415**
Fowlke, Sir Francis, Cork Francis, Mary, Limerick

Francke,Thomas, .Meath and King's Francklin, Capt. Richel., Antrim Frend, Capt. John, Limerick

Green, Thomas, Kerry, Clare, Lim'k and Wexford Gregory, Roger, Meath

Grey, Lieut. Col. John, Queen's Grice, Sir Richard, Lim' k and Kerry

Stubber's regiment continued its involvement in many more bloody and brutal battles in Ireland including the famous Battle of Clonmel mid 1650 in which Cromwell's brilliance as a General and indeed his luck almost failed him.

CROMWELL'S LETTER. "Yesterday we stormed Clonmel, to which work both officers and soldiers did as much and more than could be expected. We had, with our guns, made a breach in their works, where after a hot fight we gave back a while; but presently charged up to the same ground again. But the enemy had made themselves exceeding strong, by doubleworks and transverse, which were worse to enter than the breach; when we came up to it, they had cross-works, and were strongly flanked from the houses within their works. The enemy defended themselves against us that day, until towards the evening, our men all the while keeping up close to their breach; and many on both sides were slain. At night the enemy drew out on the other side, and marched away undiscovered to us, and the inhabitants of Clonmel sent out for a parley. Upon which articles were agreed on before we knew the enemy was gone. After the signing of the conditions we discovered the enemy to be gone, and very early this morning pursued them, and fell upon their rear of stragglers and killed above 200 besides those we slew in the storm. And on our party we had slain, Colonel Cullum, Capt. Jordan, Capt. Humphreys, and some others, and Lieut.- Colonel Grey, Lieut.- Colonel Lee, and some others are wounded. We entered Clonmel this morning, and have kept our conditions with them; the place is considerable, and very advantageous to the reducing of these parts wholly to the Parliament of England."[xxxv]

Lt Colonel John was so badly wounded he wrote his Will with his companions beside him.

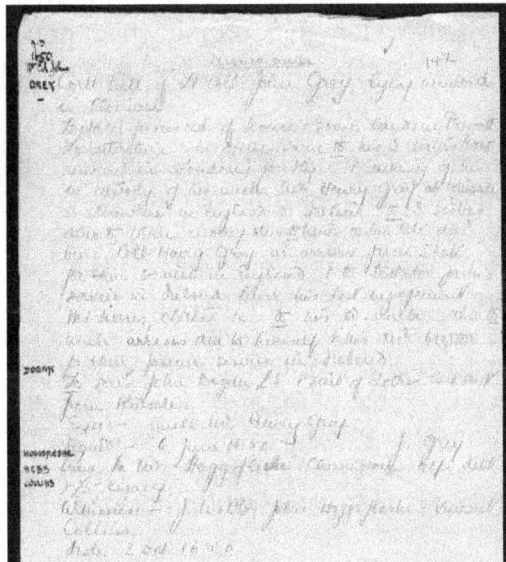

*Last (?) will of LT Coll. John Grey lying wounded in Clonmel.*

*Testator possessed of house and some land in Prescott, Leicestershire. He devises [bequest] same <u>to</u> his 3 sisters, (now resident in London) jointly and money of his in custody of his uncle Mr Henry Grey at Kinsale or elsewhere in England or Ireland, <u>to</u> his 3 sisters also <u>to</u> them money due <u>to</u> him or his late deceased brother: Coll Henry Grey due arrears from State for their services in England and to testator for his services in Ireland since his last engagement, his horse, clothes etc <u>to</u> his (?). Uncle also <u>to</u> uncle arrears due to himself and his deceased brother for their former service in Ireland.*

*<u>For</u> service, John Dogan £5 and suit of clothes last sent from Kinsale.*

*Executor: - Uncle Mr. Henry Grey*

*AD 1650 Lt Col John Grey*

*Signed – 6<sup>th</sup> June 1650. J Grey*

*Leaves to William Hoggsfleshe Surgeon(?) 40 (shillings) debt and £5 legacy Witnesses – J Webb, John Hoggsfleshe, Vincent Collins*

*Prob[?] ?ole 2 Oct 1650*

The only puzzling aspect to this document is the last word which could read Prob [Probate] 2 Oct 1650 and as such its meaning remains an open question for further research. However, it seems unlikely that there were two Lt Colonel John Grey's in the Army at Clonmel so it may be assumed that he did indeed recover from his wounds and survived.

Stubber's regiment moved south to Kinsale for winter and from July to October 1651 the regiment was at the siege of Limerick during which nearly 2000 of Parliament's men died from battle and illness, including Cromwell's son-in-law, Major General Ireton.

The regiment then moved north to Galway in May 1652, and after a long and gruelling siege, the city finally gave in to the Parliamentary forces. To understand what happened next, it may help to set the scene as it was on the day Stubber's troops entered the city. Here was a regiment which was known to have a reputation for lawlessness, disorder, thievery, generally a mix of misfits. The men had been on the move in Ireland for nearly three years and had been active in some of the bloodiest, brutal fighting in the War. They were rarely paid but had been promised land and whatever they could plunder. The war they knew was at an end, Ireland was well and truly defeated and they were now at the far reaches of the land itself. Colonel, Stubber was pretty much focused on his own needs and personal power. Galway itself was desolate after months without food, water and now in defeat.

It takes little imagination to appreciate what occurred after the troops marched through the town beating their drums. Stubber's time as Governor of Galway is also well documented and hence it is unnecessary to spell out his actions in greater detail here. Suffice to say Stubber's 'reign of terror' until 1657 was a well-deserved title which, incidentally, included slavery.

[2] Wright's *History of Ireland*, vol. ii. p. 86. Stubber was afterwards governor of Galway. Under pretence of taking up vagrants and idle persons, he made frequent excursions by night with armed troops into the country, and seized upwards of a thousand people, often without discrimination of rank or condition, whom he transported to the West Indies, and there had sold as slaves. Hardiman's *History of Galway*, p. 134. It was suspected that Stubber was the executioner of Charles I. *Ibid*, p. 12.

xxxvii

Presumably if Gray had stayed with the regiment then his life as a soldier would almost certainly have ended when it was disbanded in 1655. A prime motive for his military involvement was most likely the promise of land and would have necessitated his service in the army until it was no longer required. The setting down of the army was effected in three great disbanding's and assignments of land to the soldiery, which took place in September, 1655, and in July and November, 1656. The following list concerns the first of these disbanding's : "On 18

August, 1655, Lieut. –General Ludlow's, Sir Charles Coote's, Colonel Pretty's regiments of horse, and Colonel Ingoldsby's regiment of dragoons, and Colonel Axtels', Colonel Stubber's, and Colonel Clarke's regiments of foot, and some non-regimental companies were disbanded. About sixty troops and companies were then satisfied. In the list will be found not only the equalization of the several baronies, but the names of the different captains, troops, and companies, they were set out to in succession.[xxxviii]

This must have been a significant time for Gray regardless of his length of service. Soon his life was to lead into farming and the turmoil's of domestication.

# BOX TWO: LIFE BEYOND THE MILITARY, SPOILS OF WAR

In August 1652, Parliament passed the Act for the Settlement of Ireland and effectively confiscated virtually all the land from former Irish owners and blanketed the country with an apartheid culture of segregation and discrimination based on race and religion. Indigenous Irish were either killed, enslaved or exiled to the poverty of Connaught in the West. They were given two years to move, often with only the chattels they could carry. It is interesting to note that prior to the war, 60% of Ireland was owned by the Irish but by the time of the restoration of Charles II, this had declined to 20% and the population had declined by nearly half.[xxxix]

The English Parliament now had large tracts of land available to fulfill its promise to their soldiers. This included an allocation to Lt Colonel John Gray in the beautiful area of the Ballycurragh, a townland adjoining Aghancon and The Leap in Offaly. It should be noted that the name has had many changes over time. Its original Gaelic is Baile Mhic Mhurchú, meaning 'the town on the plain' (townland). It was also known as Ballimoragh.[xl]

[xli]

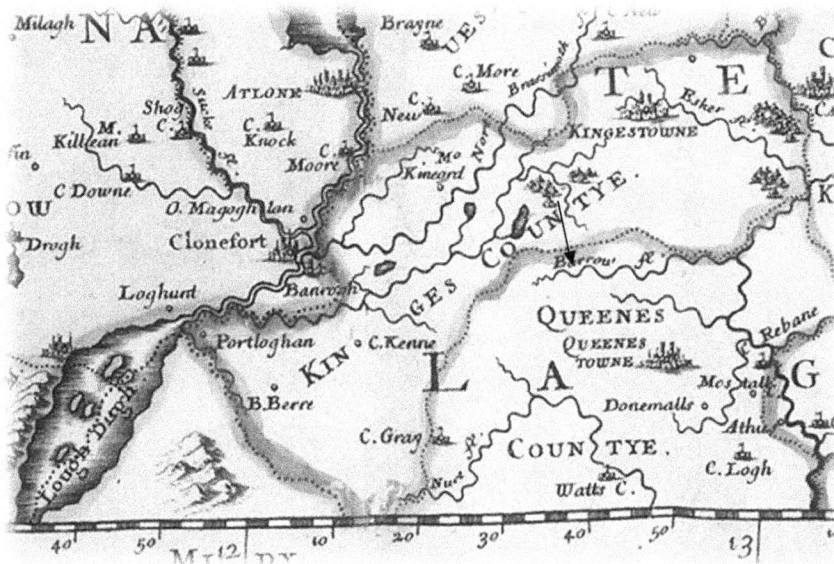

*Figure 58 Creator: Sanson; Boazio; Speed 1665 Partie meridio.le du royaume d'Irlande Publisher: chez l'autheur From Oldmapsonline. Public Domain*

Paddy Murray points to the 1664 map showing Grace Castle, Watts Castle and Castle Gray in Roscomroe and when the overlay maps were compared they matched the site identified as Roscomroe Manor. The symbol Castle with a flag raised denotes a well garrisoned and secured area for the Cromwell forces although in reality no actual Castle existed at the site indicated by most of the symbols. In Roscomroe they had the Manor, farm buildings etc plus an everlasting supply of spring water from the seven springs. A large number of Cromwellian forces also settled in the Protestant parish of Aghancon and other areas adjoining Roscomroe, during the penal times 1600s and 1700s. A few natives clung to the Mountain edges; they walked the King's Highway at the pain of death and if seen in the field they were fair game. There was also an area called 'The File' where strangers were allowed to pass through the area and a field aptly called 'The Spike' used to defend to the pass. A little more mysterious is Boherna-pucha, road of the devil, believed to have earned its name from suspicious activities undertaken there.

Paddy Murray also believes that Colonel Gray was one the of the Cromwellian Commissioners charged with executing the 1652 Act of Settlement Land that redis-tributed Irish land to the soldiers and others during this time. Land and back pay were important issues for many soldiers and once again Gray is mentioned in the Parlia-mentary proceedings on August 12 1657. He was most certainly a powerful and influential figure in the area and appears on several maps at this location from 1654 onwards, and for at least three decades.

> ♣ Same.       SAME of COL. PETER STUBBER.
>
> Nearly £2,000 was due to him, Capt. John Gray and Col. Henry Gray, for service done in Ireland before 1649 : in satisfaction for which the petitioner, on the revolt of Lord Inchiquin, obtained an order out of rebels' lands in Ireland. Other sums are due to him as the purchaser of debentures for service in England, but he could not receive them as he was serving in Ireland.
>
> Prays for satisfaction out of the town and lands of Loughrea in Ireland—which are now in his possession—or out of concealed lands in England, or otherwise. *P. ½.  No order recorded.  Ibid. p. 9.*

xlii

The fact that he is listed as Captain may be because the citation refers to his service before 1649 at which time he may well have been a captain. It is clear though he was granted land and he is listed in the 'Soldiers of the Commonwealth' as being in King's County.

xliii

## Life in Ballycurragh

When Lt. Colonel John Gray (retired) arrived at his land in Ballycurragh, he was likely to have been met with the icy silence of despair and devastation for miles around. Ironically, this was largely due to the actions of his army compatriots when, 'in the spring of 1650, General John Reynolds marched from Kilkenny with twelve thousand men to subdue Laois and Offaly. He destroyed everything in his path – castles, monasteries and churches. When his army had passed through, there was nothing left only desolation.'[xliv]

It is perhaps revealing to picture the area a few years before the war, in a description written by a rather incredulous English traveller in 1600;

It seems incredible, that by so barbarous inhabitants, the ground should be so manured, the fields so orderly fenced, the Townes so frequently inhabited, the high-waies and paths so well beaten the reason was that the Queen's forces during these warres never till then came among them.[xlv]

This was indeed a dangerous and treacherous area in which to live. While Dublin and other cities were relatively safe, the countryside was a different matter with rebel fighters, who in their minds were still at war. The mountainous and wooded terrain around Slieve Bloom was a favourite hideaway for armed bands of Irish fighters whose sole intent was to drive the English out of Ireland. There were frequent attacks on the new settlers, who were isolated and few in numbers. Added to this, Gray and his family would have been in fear of wolves and other animals from the forest. In fact, the bounty paid for a wolf was the same as that for an Irish rebel!

> The last wolf killed in Ireland was around 1786 Dr Kieran Hickey 2013 'Wolves and Cultural History' Four Corners Press

The most famous or infamous Rebel leaders remain an influential part of local folk lore. Names such as Owen Flanagan from Clonlee; Art Molloy, Drumcullen; Daniel Dunne, Clonaslee and Anthony Carroll, Tulla. There were many more over the centuries including; William Hogan, Newtown William Carroll, Longford John Carroll, Tulla Danial Carroll, Longford Donnell Oge Molloy, Drumcullen Edward Brennan, Newtown.

Danger was ever present for many generations to come. Thirty years later after the Battle of the Boyne, fleeing soldiers rampaged through the area. The second-generation Grays and their English compatriots were now faced with an insidious and vengeful enemy – the Irish Repartees (rebel Irish fighters) were boosted by the influx of fleeing soldiers from the battles. They had nothing to lose. Their only hope had been with the Catholic armies of King James II and his French allies. Once routed, they had to flee for their lives, homeless, stateless and desperate, swarming through the countryside including Ballybritt and the area around Ballycurragh. Many houses were burned, stock was taken and English were killed during this time. The present- day tranquility of the quiet and beautiful countryside belies such dangers and human sorrow.

The few locals left were peasants allowed to stay so they could work for the new masters of the land. They spoke their own language and were unlikely to have any desire to learn English, and vice versa for Gray and his neighbours. Their religion was abhorrent to the English and their culture was dismissed and repressed. Most of the men were killed or exiled, leaving mainly older people, women and children whose animosity would have been palpable.

The idea of the Plantation of a Protestant population in Ireland was ill conceived and doomed to fail. It takes more than land to make a productive farm. Most soldiers were given small tracts of land with no money or farming implements and after years of war few had the know-how to create a productive farm. Coupled with this Parliament had outlawed marriage to Catholics and should any succumb to temptation they faced the prospect of public flogging. One would imagine there would be a dearth of suitable Protestant girls in the rural backwaters of Ireland and hence most of the Cromwellian soldiers left. The Gray family did not.

There were probably several compelling reasons for this. As a Colonel Gray's land grant would have been substantial, most likely with a house and some remaining tenant farmers. It seems likely that John Gray was a younger son with little prospect of inheritance, hence his devotion to the Army and prospects of fortune through the rewards of service and plunders of war. Mary, his wife, had grown up in Ireland with her family in Dublin and even though her father came from London and returned there

at the end of his life, her formative years were certainly cultivated on Irish soil. Whatever the reason, the family stayed and prospered through land grants and their Protestant prominence. Gray and a few others maintained control for generations to come with the aid of oppressive laws and brutal enforcement.

There were some positives. Sword making had become a major growth industry for this area. This was due to the availability of trees for the furnaces and with time the swordsmiths bought up as much land as they could from the soldiers who were often only too pleased to leave with money in their pockets. Gray may have prospered through selling land or trees, certainly by the end of the 1600s the vast majority of the forests had been felled.

Lt Colonel John Gray had now gone from soldier to defender. As a Cromwellian, his task was to kill, destroy, burn, enslave and extract the land from the Irish for greater good of Parliament and the Protestant faith. He had no personal stake in the venture except for the promise of land and future prosperity. How his life had changed! Now he was a land owner, with a house, wife, and children and stock to protect. Material benefits of conquest were evident and intertwined with that of family and a fresh emotional commitment.

*Regardless of the political, military and social events swirling around him the primary concern for the family was to protect their children.*

The location of his house has been identified by Paddy Murray, a well- respected local historian. The area is now within a new forest reserve. (Presumably without wolves or rebels!) The map below shows the location which fits exactly with the description in family notes recorded by his great grandson, Basil Gray. As noted in the Family Note Book

He settled at Ballycurragh, near the Leap or Leep, King's Co. Barony of Ballybritt. Six miles from Birr...buried at Aughan-Con. People currently living in the area, according to Paddy Murray, refer to Gray's place as island (or Ireland?) house so it remains in local folklore.

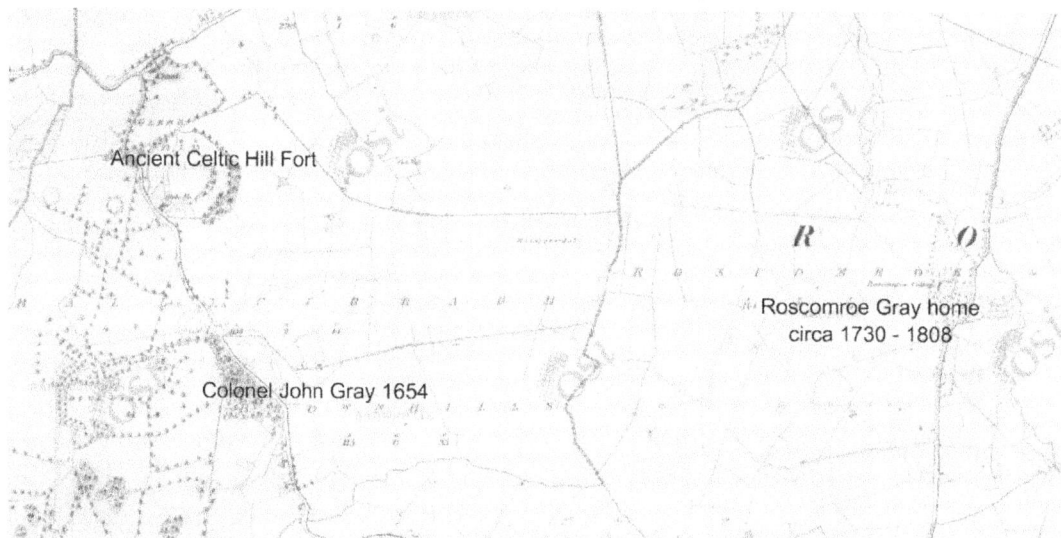

Figure 59  Adapted from the 1837 Ordnance Map

XXV

## Family Life – Basil Family

Gray, according to Basil Gray's family notes, married three times, one marriage was to 'the daughter of Colonel Basil,

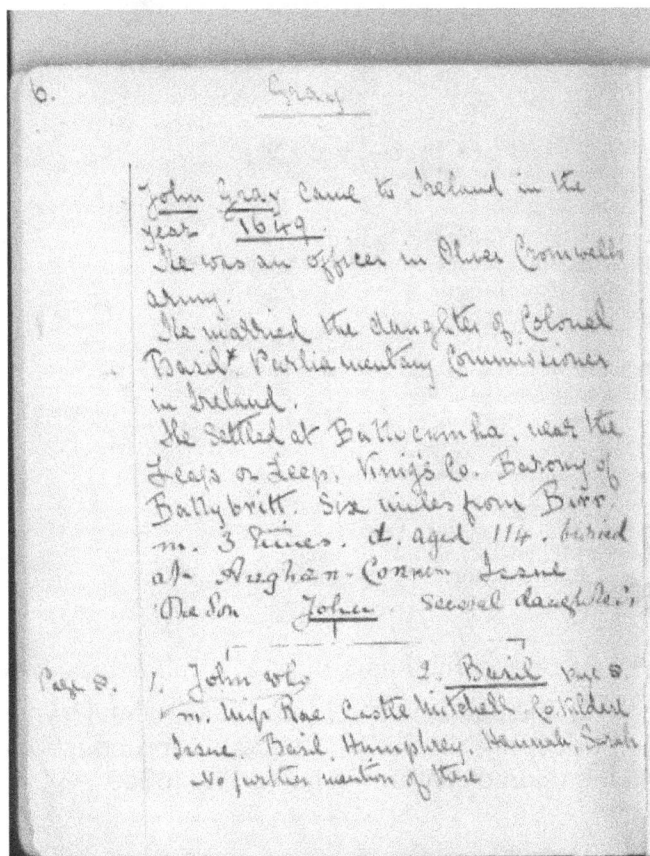

Parliamentary Commissioner in Ireland'. While his marriage to William Basil's daughter is well documented there are no records for the remaining two and it is conceivable that another branch of the family may also exist.

William Basil's first appointment to Ireland seems to have been as early as 1646. He was a Lawyer and not a Colonel.

*Resolved*, &c. That this House doth approve of *William Basil*, of *Lincoln's Inn*, Esquire, to go into *Ireland* with the Lord Lieutenant of *Ireland*, in the Place and Employment of the King's Attorney General for that Kingdom; and do order, That the Solicitor General for *England* do prepare a Grant for that Place, to the said Mr. *William Basil*, in usual Form, to pass the Great Seal of *England*: And that the Commissioners of the Great Seal for the time being do pass the said Grant accordingly.

The Lords Concurrence to be desired herein.28 January, 1646. [xlvi]

Figure 1 Page from the Grey Family Note Book

During the following decade or so he appears to have been very successful and also managed to survive through the Restoration period when he was granted a general pardon under the Letters Patent on 6<sup>th</sup> Feb 1661 [xlvii]

CATALOGUE                    348

early in 1659; was appointed baron of the Exchequer later in that year; died in Dublin 1688.

1659 **William Basil**;
was fifth son of Martin Basil of Colchester in Essex; entered Lincoln's Inn 1628; was called to the bar 1636; succeeded to property in Ireland 1642; became a bencher of his inn 1648; acted as a trustee of money raised for the Irish service same year; went to Ireland as attorney-general 1649; became a member of the King's Inns 1650; was said by Lord Deputy Fleetwood to be a very able, honest man 1654; became chief justice of the Upper Bench 1659; resided near Dublin at Donnycarny, now known as Marino; died in London in or before 1693; married twice, firstly Anne, fifth daughter of Sir John King and sister of the first Lord Kingston, and secondly the Hon. Mary Caulfeild, daughter of William, second Lord Charlemont, and left issue.

xlviii

Basil acquired the estate of Donnycarney as a bribe in 1653 and built the first Donnycarney House in 1659. [xlix] The estate was restored to its rightful owners after the Restoration, although it appears that Basil remained in the house and his family retained the land until the reign of William III in the late 1600s.

At that time Donnycarney House had become the residence of William Basil, who for the first nine years of the Commonwealth was attorney-general, and for the last two years chief justice of the chief place in Ireland. He belonged to an English family, of which more than one member had received legal training at Lincoln's Inn, but he was connected by property with the north of Ireland, and married as a first wife a sister of the first Lord Kingston, and as a second a sister of the third Lord Charlemont. Shortly before the Restoration the inhabitants of full age on the Donnycarney lands were returned as eight of English and six of Irish descent, Basil and one Peter Vaughan being the only persons of position ; and after the Restoration Donnycarney House, which was still occupied by Basil, appears as rated in 1664 for eight and in 1667 for fifteen hearths.[1]

Before the Restoration Drumcondra, which included possibly Clonturk and Drishoge, had a population of over a hundred persons of full age, twenty-seven being English and eighty-six Irish, the chief

[1] Records of Dublin, iii, 458, 467, 468, 479 ; Prerogative Will.
[2] Lodge's " Peerage," iii, 138, 233 ; " Lincoln's Inn Admissions " ; Prerogative Will ; Census of 1659 ; Hearth Money Rolls.

Basil was married twice, first to Anne King, daughter of Sir Robert King and Frances Ffolliott. Anne died in 1652 without issue.

The six daughters of Sir Robert and Frances were : Catherine and Anne, who died young.—Mary, who married, first, William, son and heir of Sir Robert Meredyth, of Greenhills, County Kildare, Baronet, and secondly, William Earl of Denbigh and Desmond. She died before 1662, and was buried in St. Michan's church, Dublin.—Elizabeth died unmarried—and Anne, who married William Basil of Donnycarney, the Irish Attorney-General during the Protectorate. She died in February, 1652, and was also buried in St. Michan's.

His second marriage was to Mary Caulfeild (also spelt Caulfield) as shown below;

William Basil whose family had acquired Bingley Estates in Lifford County Donegal in the 1630's who married the daughter of a prominent Fermanagh [lii]planter, Sir William Caulfeild ...[liii]

Sir William Caulfeild was the Sheriff of Tryone, 2nd Baron of Charlemont (dbt 08.10.1587, d 04.12.1640) and married to Mary King (d 1663, daughter of Sir John King of Bolye Abbey). Their daughter's name was also Mary (b 1625 d 24.09.1668) and buried the following day at St Michaels, Dublin[liv]

It is interesting to note that William Basil's two wives (Anne King then Mary Caulfeild) were first cousins, being both granddaughters of Sir John King of Boyle. The Caulfeild and King families were closely associated for many years.[lv] Mary Basil (nee Caulfeild) and William Basil must have been married sometime after 1652. They had four children: Martin Caulfeild (d 1735), Mary, Edmund, and Anne.

Gray may have married either Mary or Anne although if the latter, then the union would have been be a few years later. Considering the age difference a reasonable assumption is that he chose the elder daughter. The timing here is interesting: Mary must have been born in the mid-1650s and would have become of marriageable age very early, perhaps the later part of the 1660s, at which stage Gray was probably well into his late 40s or older if he were a young ensign in 1645.

The union made sense for both families. Presumably the pool of young, eligible men at that time was somewhat limited in Ireland by reason of religion, location, social status, wealth and because so many Protestant families had left Ireland after the 1641 rebellion and the turmoil of the times. It should also be remembered that Mary's mother had died at 43 when the children were all quite young and her father, William, would most certainly have determined whom his daughters were to marry – it is doubtful that girls had much control over their destiny. Gray was eminently suited: Basil and Gray were both Presbyterian and aristocratic. Gray had land and was financially sound and both men held similar political and moral values. It was in effect a perfect match despite the disparity in age. The couple produced a son and heir, John, and several daughters whose names have slipped into the void of history. As for John Gray, the final note from Basil Gray, his grandson, reads, 'died aged 114, buried at Aughancon.' (FNB) The latter is most certainly true while the former – improbable? Suffice to say, the rest of Basil's notes are essentially true.

One generation fades while another begins...

We take with us throughout our lifetime a myriad of memories, family stories and folklore especially from our childhood. When the Grey families stepped ashore in Van Diemen's Land each one bought with them their own personal recollections of their home in Ireland. As time went by these memories would evolve and diminish or grow in exaggeration. Some stories were passed on for future generations to relish or discard, others were lost with their generation.

Their culture was Anglo-Irish embracing all the associated values, beliefs and history of the small community in and around the district of Roscomroe but also more generally other parts of King's County.

Fortunately, Paddy Murray and Paddy Heaney have provided a delightful and fascinating insight into this part of Ireland. Their writing is like a kaleidoscope through time with so many stories, interesting anecdotes and actualities and some may well have been embedded into the thoughts and memories of the Grey family. Reading these allows a far greater understanding of the family and the cognizance they bought with them to the isolated cluster of settlers in the Fingal Valley. They were far away from the world they knew so well but many of their memories and recollections, mingled with those outlined below, would remain untainted by time for the rest of their lives.

However only three Gray families left Ireland, leaving behind brothers, sisters cousins and grandparents. These continued to live in the area for many generations and Paddy has managed to locate several branches who were still farming a century or so later, including names such as Fawcett, Payne and of course Gray.

### Welcome to Roscomroe.Roscomroe

Compiled by Paddy Murray and Paddy Heaney

I (Paddy Murray) was born in Roscomroe where I have lived most of my life. I heard stories of the past from both sides (Catholic and Protestant) which always conflicted and were very vague, by not knowing or not wishing to tell the truth we will never know. The mystery of Roscomroe deepened in my mind especially after meeting local historian, Pat Cordial, in 1963/4 and listening to his stories and knowledge of the area.

After Ian Broinowski wrote to me regarding the Gray family I contacted Paddy Heaney who is well versed in Roscomroe history seeking help to trace the Gray name in Roscomroe. Paddy had never heard the name Gray associated in the Roscomroe, oh, but what a story was to emanate from our studies.

---

Roscomroe is a small hamlet of just a few houses, a school and the relic of a medieval church and is located in the south of County Offaly in central Ireland.

County Offaly

Geashill

Birr        Kinitty
         Roscomroe
Ballycuragh      Slieve Bloom MTS

## Roscomroe Manor

The only visualisation we have of the Manor at Roscomroe is from Kate Dougharty who at the time of writing had in her possession a painting of the original building. She describes it thus: 'Built solidly, two storeys of blue stone, it had cream-pointed, round-topped mullioned windows and on the roof were two pepper-pot rooms. The chimney stacks too were a curious and interesting shape. The wings at each end of the house made it almost crescent-shaped and gave the impression that they held out welcoming arms to any relations and friends who came to visit the family. There was always room for them.'

The picture below is an artist's impression of the building and gives a sense of modest grandeur and authority. It seems likely it was seen as a bastion of Protestant influence for centuries.

Figure 2  Artist impression of the Grey Manor and Church (by Killian Donoghue 2017)

We know the layout of the estate from old maps and some relics which still exist. We have for instance stone left on site including mullions, cornice, corbel and lock stone which is still present and no doubt the chiseled stone that matches part of the house described by Kate Dougharty.

The map below shows the layout of the estate with the road passing Roscomroe cottage, the location of the high pillars and the church.

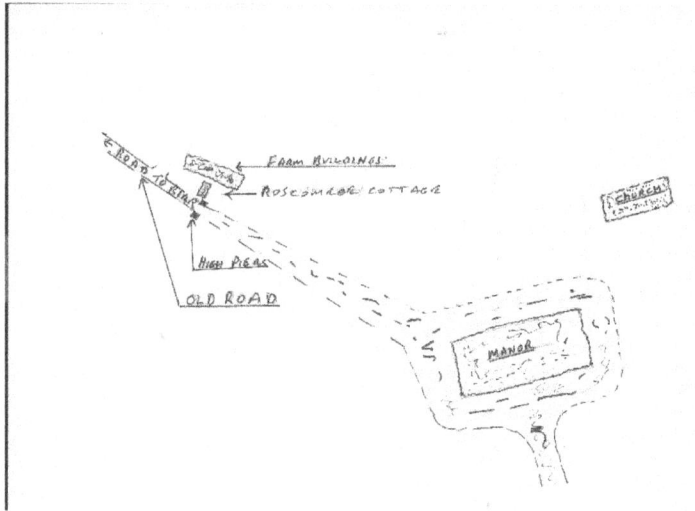

Figure 62 Roscomroe Manor Layout – Paddy Murray

This photo shows the present day site with the church in the background and both myself (Paddy Murray) and Paddy Heaney.

Figure 63 Site of Roscomroe Manor - showing Paddy Murray and Paddy Heaney

The lay-out map from 1837 shows Roscomroe Cottage existing, the Church in ruins and the location of the Manor ruins which were finally excavated during the 1950s /60s. Both Manor and Church, have a southern aspect and some senior locals also believe that a shop existed in these parts.

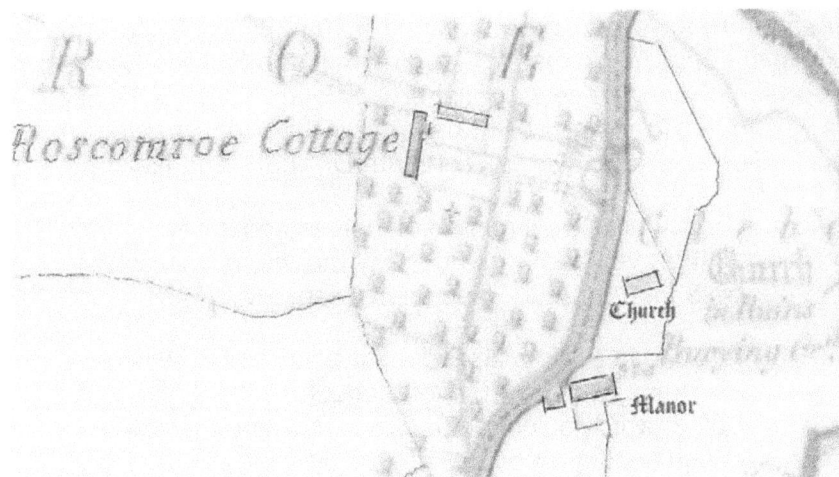

Figure 64 Map showing main features of Roscomroe

Figure 65 Roscomroe Cottage - photo curtesy of Paddy Murray

The high pier, last vestige of the Roscomroe Manor, has now succumbed to time and traffic, the rubble still remains in Flanagan's field, owner of Roscomroe Cottage. In the background is Roscomroe Bridge, the pier probably witnessed the comings and goings to the Gray home.
(*Photo taken by P Murray 1980*)

### Manor History

Roscomroe Manor was the rectory for the church and dates back to the early 1600s or before. The first Vicar in Roscomroe was William Wevill who was awarded Rectory and vicarage of Roscomroe, including thirty acres of land, on the 25th of February, 1621 for his support as minister

of religion. He was described as a good preacher and a man of good life and conversation, cure [of souls] served by himself, it seems that the Rectory/Vicarage was ready for occupation. Oliver Grace was Bishop and patron, whose family held vast amounts of land and had the livings of 18 parishes. Other Vicars to follow were Thomas Smith A.B., Gerrot Grace, Pierce Callanan, Denteth, and Nelson.

Thomas Smith, Vicar of Roscomroe, was robbed of horses, colts, mares and books during the 1641 rebellion It proves he had a house of means, possible stone walls and slated roof, the probable forerunner to Roscomroe Manor.lvi

John Grace, invariably referred to as an Irish Protestant, had the Crown lease of the Abby of Nenagh for 21 years. On the 20th of August 1660, the rectory, Churches, Chapels and Tithes all of which belonged to Grace, forming the estate of the Abby and Monastery of Nenagh, was granted to Robert Boyle for 21 years from the 17th of April 1662. The tax from Roscomroe was 1s and 11d.lvii

Basil, Lt John Gray's grandson, was the first of the Gray family to move into the Manor in circa 1730. According to the FNB he had 'resided for several years at Capanara in Ossory and removed hence to Roscomroe, one mile from his father's place in Ballycurragh' Basil married Elizabeth Carr.

Basil had five children, William b 1732, Humphrey b 1744, John b1746, Hannah, and Elizabeth. Humphrey's older brother William, left for Garrycastle and left him as the natural heir to Roscomroe. After retiring early from the Army, Humphrey returned to the life of Gentleman farmer.

### Humphrey

Humphrey's first child was Basil, born in 1768 at Roscomroe two years after his marriage to Anne (Nee Clugston). Humphrey's second marriage was to Sarah French and their second son Humphrey was born in 1780 and was destined for V.D.L. His emotional attachment to Roscomroe was clearly strong and his vivid and accurate recollections were passed onto later generations and subsequently incorporated in the story by his great granddaughter, Kate Dougharty.

| GRAY | Hannah | otherwise Fawcet, wife of John | Kilbeg, Kings Co | P 1 | 06 June 1808 | Lands at Roscomroe, Kings Co from Gray to Grace |
|------|--------|--------------------------------|------------------|-----|--------------|-------------------------------------------------|

Figure 66 Section of deed showing land at Roscomroe from Gray to Grace.

It would appear that Roscomroe was sold in 1808 to the Grace family which is perhaps understandable. Humphrey had recently married and was making a career in the Army as did most of his siblings so once their father died perhaps no one was able or willing to move in Roscomroe.

What else we know about Roscomroe?

There is a stretch of land from Roscomroe to Ballybritt along the Ballybritt River known as the File, where in the distant past the traveller, friend or foe wishing to move North or South had to pass through this narrow ravine, over looked by Lissanerin, a place often used for military parades and sports grounds. There is a field at the Roscomroe end and aptly named Spike and formed some sort of defence.

The English may occupied the Manor/Vicarage and the farm buildings that were

Figure 3 Humphrey Grey b 1744 and father to Humphrey also born at Roscomroe in 1780 who travelled to VDL in 1829. Private collection

vacated after the 1641 rebellion, when at least six farmers (Planters) were assaulted and robbed, including Thomas Smith, the Vicar of Roscomroe.[lviii]

These may have been Tulla Castle in 1659 which had eleven English and no Irish, or Killavilla/Dungar with forteen English and four Irish. Also in close proximity there were 30 English, both near to the Queens County border and adjacent to Roscomroe belonging to the O' Carrolls, who forfeited over 4000 acres of prime land. In Birr there were 64 English, all military I presume.

Interestingly a member of the Carroll family Charles, fled to Maryland,U.S.A. in 1668 with a commission from Lord Baltimore appointing him Attorney General of Maryland where Catholics were supposedly welcome. Charles Carroll, the Settler, arrived to harsher penal laws than he left in Ireland.

Although the area is in the heart of Ely O'Carroll territory it at some stage was assigned to C. Gray for one reason or another. [lix]

Finally the land act of 1652 redistributed Irish land to soldiers and others during this time. Land and pay back was an important issue for many soldiers and once again Gray is mentioned in the Parliamentary proceedings on August the 12th 1657 and most certainly was a powerful and influential figure in the area and appears on several maps from 1654 for at least three decades. A large number of Cromwellian soldiers received land and populated the area in and around Roscomroe, especially in the newly created  Protestant parish of Aghancon in 1628.

[lx]

## Gray Families who remained in Ireland

John Gray of Roscomroe married Hannah Fawcett of Geashill in Geashill parish Church on the 21st of April 1775, they had three sons, Basil, Fawcett and John as well two daughters, Rebecca and Nchola. (suggest Nichola)

More recent records show that in the 1901 census George Payne aged 41 with his wife (Jane Frances Gray) aged 38 and children, George H. aged 4, William aged 1 and Rebeca infant, were listed in house no. 17 in Derrycooley, Geashill. In 1911 again in Derrycooley were George, head, George junior aged 14 and William aged 11.

The oldest Gray in the 1911 census was Eliza Gray 80 years old, living in Geashill with her niece in house no 4, Jane Frances Payne (nee Gray) head of house, Eliza is described as her Aunt, born 1831. The youngest Grays in Geashill were Fawcett age 37 and William age 34, in the 1911 census. The only Fawcett grave site in in Geashill. The Primary names of Basil, John, Fawcett, William and Hannah were popular names in the Geashill area all decendents of John and Hannah of Roscomroe.

John Gray of Roscomroe married Hannah Fawcett of Geashill here on the 21$^{st}$ of April 1775. BOX FOUR: REASONS TO EMIGRATE

In the mid-1820s, three Gray families chose to go to Van Diemen's Land thousands of miles away from Ireland, remote, shadowy and fraught with dangers. About as far away from their home as possible, it was a penal colony, at war with the Aborigines and a complete unknown in terms of what it had to offer. So the risks were significant, to say nothing of an outward perilous voyage of several months to actually reach the Island and that they were unlikely to ever see their homeland ever again.

Those who chose to emigrate were: William and Eleanor, James and Mary, their mother Anne Gray as well as Humphrey and Catherine Grey. Each had there own reasons for going which are a challenge to understand, especially from a distance of nearly 200 years. There are, however, some factors which help to explain their decision.

### Living in Ireland in the late 1700s

The Grays lived in turbulent times. By the end of the 1700s a myriad of secret and open societies had evolved to fight for their political and social ends. One such was the United Irishmen founded by a Presbyterian in 1791, and included Catholic citizens. At first working for political reform through peaceful campaigns and Parliament, eventually out of frustration resorted to violence and armed resistance. Other groups were secret, passionate and uncompromising, such as the White Fleet, a Catholic force, and the Protestant Mountain Rangers. Tensions grew until the 1798 Rebellion, which resulted in atrocious death and destruction throughout Ireland.

It is little wonder that Irish Catholics felt aggrieved. Since 1642, the English Protestants had systematically imposed an apartheid social and political system in Ireland. These are some examples although by no means all such laws passed by Parliament. The Penal Laws of 1695 and '97 denied Catholics any form of education, they were forced to give up arms, they could not own a horse over five pounds and if they did a Protestant could demand it for the same amount.

While the parish clergy were left in place, subject to strict rules of behavior, all 'bishops, Jesuits, friars and monks were ordered to leave the Kingdom by 1st May 1698'[lxi] Intermarriage was prohibited and land was to be divided between all children hence causing properties became smaller and unworkable. There were of course many more oppressive laws which are well documented but this shows a little of the background and reasons for the poverty and resentment by the Irish and the background to the rebellion.[lxii]

### Humphrey Grey and 1798 Rebellion

Humphrey Grey was born in 1780 and grew up with social disharmony as part of his life. He was certainly active in quelling the rebellion in 1798 as shown in the obituary written in Tasmanian papers at his death in 1868

*'He was engaged on the side of loyalty in the Irish Rebellion of 1798'.*[lxiii]

Humphrey was in his late teens and most likely was part of the Leap Independents initially started by Colonel Darby in the year of his birth. It is also possible, according to Paddy Murray that he was attached to the King's County or Cork Militia.

Figure 4 Grey Family Silver

As a young man, Humphrey lived through the troubling times. One description tells us a great deal about their everyday conditions:

Sir Charles Coote, the author of the Statistical Surveys for the King's and Queens Counties (1801), describes in shocked tones the houses of the peasants in the districts around Slieve Bloom, where men, women, children and animals were bedded down in the same single room, citing the immorality to which this practice must have given rise as an example of 'the irreclaimable barbarity, and civilization of the peasantry of Ireland';

The peasant cots are throughout miserably poor and wretched, in a few instances weather proof, yet fondly clung to by the natives, who are attached to them from custom, and perhaps from the warmth occasioned by their smoke and lowness, as they prefer living in them to neat slate lodges and farm houses. Lxiv

However, Humphrey clearly stayed firmly on the side of Loyalty and the British Army even though many of his fellow Presbyterians felt aggrieved by the injustices of the times and fought and died for liberties which were to remain elusive for well over a century. It was terrible, civil war with countless atrocities on both sides and leaving thousands of dead. Humphrey was by now well accustomed to the horrors of war.

Once the Irish had been violently and decisively put back in their place, with Ireland being unequivocally united with the Kingdom of Great Britain the family appeared to be in a celebratory mood and commissioned a full set of silver ware for the occasion. Kate Dougharty says;

The table silver, manufactured in 1801 to celebrate the Union, still belongs to us, because the Greys, glad of the event, hoped to hand it down to their descendants and used it only for weddings, parties and special occasions. A chest of silver had been brought safely from the old home. It had been especially designed in 1801, at the time of the Union of England, Ireland, Scotland and Wales and their emblems were embossed on the handles on each piece. [lxv]

## Political and social context of Ireland in the early 1820s

Ireland was despairingly poor and the next generation lived with unease and social tension. The 1798 bloody rebellion remained an ever present reminder of the possible consequences of social discontent. The Union in 1801 with Great Britain had hindered rather than helped by alienating the Protestant population far more. Direct rule from Westminster clearly had its short comings in terms of distance and influence on law making.

The Catholic movement was strong at this point with the Catholic Association's Danial O'Connell able to make significant changes to the oppressive laws which affected their community and resulting in the 1830 Catholic Emancipation Act. However, despite the changes, the English managed to thwart any real chances of social reform by simply increasing the right to vote to those with an income of two pounds to ten pounds, a move which disenfranchised 80% of the Catholic population.

There was also prejudice against the Presbyterians by English Protestants mainly because of their Scottish affiliation. It is unclear the extent to which the Gray family had leanings in this direction although no doubt they had some affiliation. Colonel John Gray had married into a Presbyterian family and Humphrey himself may have had similar beliefs and his daughter, Elizabeth married a Presbyterian lay preacher.

As with most of Ireland, King's County remained a volatile and dangerous place to live, especially for Protestant families who were still regarded with suspicion and hostility. Attacks by the 'Whiteboys', also known as the Levellers, continued in and around Doneraile, the town in which Humphrey and Catherine were married. This group had been testing the authorities since its inception at Clogheen in Co. Tipperary in 1761, with constant destruction of property, their activities often resulting in death. Such events were common throughout Ireland, clearly creating a sense of unease for any parent. The following extracts illustrate examples of the unrest.

At the early hour of eight o'clock on Tuesday night, a large party attacked the house of James FOLEY, on the lands of Carrageen, the property of A.G. CREAGH, Esq., and set fire to his house and barn in three different parts, and cut and mangled two fine cows, for no cause, but that FOLEY took the land from

Mr. CREAGH, about two years ago, and was a sober, well- conducted man. Carrageen is not more than one mile from Doneraile.

At the meeting held yesterday at Doneraile, Lord COMBERMERE was met by a numerous body of the Magistrates from different baronies. The conversation chiefly turned upon the best method of employing the police and the military force in the country, for the purpose of counteracting the terrible outrages with which that part of the country is afflicted. .... The meeting was animated in the general comments that were made upon the absolute necessity of a more rigorous enforcement of the Insurrection Act.- Lord Combermere assured the meeting that the Government was resolved to strain their power to the utmost to repress the existing insurrection.- Cork Paper.lxvi Paddy Murray describes the state of Ireland during this period in the following passage;

When Grays emigrated to V.D.L. in 1828, Ireland was going through the worst period in Irish history, after successful improvements in living conditions during the Napoleonic wars. When the wars ended in 1814 there was a complete economic slump, investments and growth stagnated. In 1816-1818 bad weather destroyed corn grain and potato crops, smallpox and typhus killed over 50-000 people, the potato crop failed again in 1821 and 1825-1830. Indian meal was imported from America and stark famine was in Munster. Through the 1830s cholera ravaged the poorest, then in 1838 the year of the big wind, snow buried cottages and cattle froze to death. And in the 1840s the great famine, which many say started 1815. The Country was over populated and evictions raged over the land at a frantic pace. A number of family's from the Ballybritt and Lissanerin area led by a Priest immigrated to America.

With this background in mind it is easy to understand why the family began to look elsewhere for their future and a better life

It is easier to understand James' and William's reason for leaving on such an adventure than it is for their older cousin (once removed) Humphrey. Both were considerably younger and had served in the army, possibly in the latter part of the Napoleonic War. As part payment for service, soldiers, were offered land in VDL. Their great grandfather, Lt Colonel John Gray, had also been granted land in Ireland for his army service. How history repeats itself! Both men had little prospect for meaningful employment or financial security in Ireland, so the thought of owning their own property, coupled with free convict labour, in a far distance land would certainly have been appealing.

## James Gray

On a more personal level, each considered their own needs and future in Ireland. James Gray was born in the mid-1790s and became a member of the 8th Regiment late in the Napoleonic War and during the post war period. He achieved the rank of Lieutenant.

Married with children by the early 1820s, rural Ireland was a poor prospect for James. He had been placed on half pay from the 25th March 1817, which, after only three years of service, provided a scant income for a young family.lxvii

| John Radenhurst | 5 Aug. 1813 | 25 Mar. |
| Brooke Young | 6 do. | do. |
| Thomas Russell | 12 do. | do. |
| James Kingsley Gray | 23 Mar. 1814 | do. |
| Y y | | *Lieutenants* |

According to Kate Dougharty, James had been promised land in the colonies for his war service. It seems likely that his family did not own land as his father Richard had been a doctor in Birr and was unlikely to have provided his children with wealth of any significance. Mrs Anne Gray (nee Kingsley), their mother, accompanied William and James to VDL, which implies that they already knew the value of their inheritance

This would have been an easy decision for James to make. For someone as impetuous as James, there really was not much of a choice but to leave Ireland and follow his older brother an adventure to another land.

## William Gray

Major William Gray was a completely different character all together. A military man, decisive, direct, opinionated and confident in social status, his unquestionable Britishness derived from the British Empire and all it stood for.

William is reminiscent of Mr Knightly in Jane Austen's *Emma*:

There is one thing, Emma, which a man can always do, if he chuses, and that is, his

### PREFACE.

In offering to the public the following pages, it may be necessary to state the motives which operated to my acceptance of that important command, which it will be their business to disclose. Though not born in the camp, nor altogether educated in the field, I have been early taught in that frankness which generally characterises the soldier, and, I trust, it will be found that, in all I describe, I have never deviated from strictly acting on that honourable and faithful basis.

I had reached the shores of Africa, in my tour of service, well remembering on my passage the labours and researches of the informed and the brave who perished in the exalted struggle of benefiting their country and the benighted Africans ; while, at the same time, I could not

duty; not by maneuvering and finessing, but by vigour and resolution.[lxviii]

Such sentiments are clearly reflected in Gray's own Preface to his book relating to his expeditions in Africa for example when he says, ' I have been early taught in that frankness which generally characterises the soldier, and I have never deviated from strictly acting on that honourable and faithful basis' In other words he was a *'man's man'* which could explain why he formed such a close relationship with Governor Arthur. Both were equally ambitious, uncompromising and rarely missed an opportunity for improving their material status.[lxix]

Later as a magistrate in Avoca, he was revered or feared, depending on which side of the law a person found themselves.[lxx]

The following section from Kate Dougharty's book sums up William's situation best of all;

Cousin William and Cousin James, her father's first cousins lived a few miles

away, at Garry Castle. The former, a Major of the 94th had gone to Africa with Mungo Park[xlvi] and had helped to discover the source of the Niger. For his services there, the Government had offered him a grant of land in any British colony, and now he was seriously considering accepting it. [lxxi]

From 1818 to 1821, Major William Gray explored western Africa on behalf of the British Government. His adventures were exciting, challenging and dangerous as well as being ill prepared and quite foolhardy. Many of his fellow officers and soldiers died during the expedition from tropical diseases and on several occasions Gray almost succumbed to severe bouts of fever. He was lucky to survive. This was no small feat

I was, therefore, reduced to the disagreeable necessity of employing a person for the sole purpose of going round the country in search of a woman slave, and which he, with much difficulty, procured, not in consequence of the scarcity of those poor wretches in the country, but of the enormous price demanded, arising no doubt from their knowledge of the obligation I was under of providing one without delay.

This transaction I could not bring myself to negotiate, as the idea alone of dealing in human flesh was more than sufficiently disagreeable to allow me to see the poor wretch, who, although only changing master, and, from what I could learn, getting a good for a bad one, was nevertheless a slave bought and sold. Osman, who had no scruples of that kind, very willingly undertook to do it for me, and I have no doubt made something by it.

with over 100 soldiers and civilians and 200 animals on the first expedition. They continued to explore from the river Gambia, through Woolli, Bondoo, Galam, Kasson, Kaarta, and Foolidoo, although they never actually reached the river Niger.

He related these adventures in a book, *Travels in Western Africa* in 1825. It is not only a fascinating tale of the times, but it also shows glimpses of Gray as a person. He certainly grappled with moral and ethical issues, although with his clearly defined sense of self and confidence in the righteousness of the British ethos and practicalities of situations, he habitually found satisfactory resolutions.

For example at one point, a soldier accidentally killed a woman while cleaning his gun. After quelling a potentially violent response from the local tribe, Gray received a message from the chief to say that he accepted it was an accident although he would require a new slave woman to take her place.[lxxii] Gray was pragmatic enough to concur although his final comments are quite revealing;

*Thus terminated an unfortunate affair which, although wholly providential, was certainly of such an un-pleasant nature as to cause deep regret to all our party; but which did not appear to make any more impression on the minds of the natives,*

*than if the deceased had been a bullock; so little is the life of a slave noticed in that country.*

On another occasion the book describes Gray's reaction to an apparent atrocity in Africa, where he showed some reflection and thought, albeit within defined moral parameters.[lxxiii]

An assessment of Gray's African expedition by Dane Kennedy from George Washington University is scathing and directly to the point;

It also found that it had entered an environment plagued by wars between neighboring states, making passage through the region nearly impossible. Grey finally swallowed his pride and appealed for rescue to the French, whose influence in the region the British had sought to supplant. The forlorn party finally returned to the coast a full six years after the original expedition had set out. The long endeavor had proven a costly, ignominious failure.[lxxiv]

He goes on to say that both this and other equally disastrous British expeditions into Africa were wiped from the collective memory which may also help to understand why William felt it prudent to move as far away from Home as possible!

It was destroyed about twelve months before by the people of Bondoo, in one of their plundering excursions, and many of its inhabitants were either killed or made prisoners (slaves), a fate but too common in this country, where the strongest party always finds an excuse for making war on the weaker, not unfrequently carrying off whole towns of miserable inoffensive beings, without either any previous intimation of their hostile intentions, or indeed any cause given by those wretched objects of their avaricious encroachments. On all such occasions, the only object in view is the attainment of money, as they call it, and in this they succeed by selling their unfortunate fellow-creatures, and, what is still more unnatural, their compatriots, to slave-dealers.

A multitude of ideas, bringing with them the conviction of how much Englishmen, and indeed all civilized nations, are favoured by Divine Providence, in enjoying freedom and security against such unwarranted and barbarous practices, rushed on my mind, as we surveyed the silent and awful remains of some human bodies which lay outside the walls of this once respectable and no doubt happy town, the inhabitants of which were torn by unrelenting savages from that native spot, so dear to all mankind. Even the strongest ties of nature riven asunder, and all this to gratify the brutal desires of some neighbouring tyrant, or to enrich a set of savages, who are daily exposed to a similar fate themselves, at least as long as they can find people ready to purchase their unnatural booty.

Changing environments can influence moral perspectives. A few years later, Major William was an active participant in the Black War against the Aboriginal people of Trouwunna population around Avoca. However in this context, Gray's need for self- preservation and land ownership appear to be his prime motivator. Although he never deviated from his adherence to the fundamental values of the British Empire.

By 1825, William's future was tenuous, with few realistic prospects in the army or in Ireland. Employment prospects for a retired major and African explorer were somewhat limited especially now that he had a young family. The offer of land anywhere in the Empire as reward for his services in the army and exploration of the Niger River, offered real and exciting possibilities.

lxxv

Figure 5  Image of cere-
monial attire featured in

*l.x. 1825*

TRAVELS

IN

WESTERN AFRICA,

IN THE YEARS 1818, 19, 20, AND 21,

FROM THE

RIVER GAMBIA, THROUGH WOOLLI, BONDOO, GALAM,
KASSON, KAARTA, AND
FOOLIDOO, TO THE RIVER NIGER.

BY

MAJOR WILLIAM GRAY,

AND THE LATE

STAFF SURGEON DOCHARD.

WITH A MAP, DRAWINGS, AND COSTUMES, ILLUSTRATIVE
OF THOSE COUNTRIES.

Quod si deficiant vires, audacia certè
Laus erit in magnis, et voluisse sat est.
PROP.

LONDON:

JOHN MURRAY, ALBEMARLE STREET.

MDCCCXXV.

*51 6.*

The decision for William again was an easy (
in VDL and the prospect of material gain would have been an opportunity too alluring to resist.

## Humphrey Grey

Humphrey's reasons are a little more puzzling and subtle. He was much older and in fact he would have been close to 50 by the time he reached VDL. Ironically, he outlived his young cousins by many years. He had worked for nearly thirty years with the Commissariat, which was the supply branch of the Army and as shown below, his final position was as a store keeper. His superannuation was a modest payout of £34.19.7.[lxxvi]

However Humphrey clearly had private wealth, enabling him to send the older girls to finishing school in Paris, to help pay for the passage on *Letitia* and to bring three servants with him to VDL. Kate Dougharty provides a clue to their predicament:

Uncle Quain (on the maternal side) was a clever barrister and had always had the family affairs in hand. He had been warning them lately that Irish stocks, from which most of their income was derived, were low on the market, and that owing to the potato blight, some of their tenant farmers were unable to pay their rents, and were not taking fresh leases, but were emigrating instead.[lxxvii]

Concern regarding Irish stocks was a compelling factor, although it should be noted that the potato blight did not start until many years later, in 1845. It is interesting that Humphrey was a land owner as well.

So what would induce a quiet, contemplative person such as Humphrey Grey to take a delicate wife and children to the far-flung island of Van Diemen's Land? Perhaps it was his desire to provide a more secure future for his children, maybe a sense of adventure or to use a modern colloquialism, Humphrey may have been experiencing a "mid-life crisis"! He arrived with sufficient finances to establish his family in a comfortable lifestyle; although a grant of prime farming land at Avoca would undoubtedly have helped. Their house at Eastbourne is certainly far superior to that of either James or William. Humphrey was a businessman and very successful throughout his life. When looking at it in a prudential light emigration to VDL was an obvious decision to make from a financial perspective as it provided many more opportunities in farming and material security. Humphrey built up his assets and wealth steadily throughout his life, and was able to provide substantial properties for his children and their families. For Humphrey the choice to emigrate was both opportune and made business sense.

Humphrey and Catherine Grey arrived in Hobart on the Brig Ann on the 8th July 1829 to join Humphrey's cousins, William and James at Avoca. Humphrey used the name Grey rather than Gray and had done so for generations. Certainly his marriage documents contain this spelling. Humphrey was a cautious, thoughtful man with a keen sense of business with maturity on his side and had accumulated some considerable wealth before deciding to emigrate.

Catherine (Kate) Mahony, daughter of Andrew, from Mallow in Co Cork was born in 1779 and married Humphrey at Donervaile County in Feb 1808.[lxxviii]

---

| 1812] | HIBERNIAN MAGAZINE. | 189 |
|---|---|---|

,,  Humphrey, Donevaile = Mahony, C., d. of Andrew,
Mallow                        Feb. 1806   125

---

Humphrey and Catherine were at a different stage of their lives than the younger families already in Avoca. Both in their late forties they were accompanied by adult children in their new life in VDL. Margaret at 22, Humphrey 20, and Catherine 15 with two younger children Henrietta 9 and Lysbeth 7[lxxix].

Although Humphrey had taken longer to decide whether to emigrate than his more impetuous and spirited cousins he soon became committed and set about planning their exodus from Ireland.

### The Journey

This probably reflected more on Humphrey's nature than anything but the potential for a better life in the colonies must have eventually persuaded him to commit and so, on the 19th of July 1828 the Grey family set sail to VDL on the *Letitia*. Humphrey had commissioned the ship with several other families including;

(Commander) William Moriarty from Summer Hill in Cork, John Gee of Rathmolyn, Co. Meath, Henry Gee, his cousin, all with their families and some with servants, following, like Edward Conyngham of Dublin, siblings already settled on the other side of the world. The irascible Joseph Henry Moore, son of the Earl of Drogheda, and his family, from Dublin; Richard Popham of Bandon, Co. Cork; Dr Jonathan Clerke, his brother Alexander, with his wife, married only days before in Skibbereen, Co. Cork on 19 June, gathered their belongings. Mrs Ann Weston, together with her son, joined the group, setting out to join her husband, Superintendant of the Hyde Park Barracks inSydney.[lxxx]

The journey though well planned failed dismally once it reached St Jago. The Captain's seamanship and sobriety left much to be desired and the crew were inexperienced and ineffectual. At the port of St Jago the ship was inadequately secured against an oncoming storm and was crushed upon the rocks before sinking.

The event was not reported in Dublin until a month later when;

*Wreck of the Letitia, Capt. Clements.*

*" We have been favoured with the perusal of a letter fom Porto Prago, Island of St Jago and another dated 22nd of October last, from Rio de Janiero, stating some of the particulars of the unfortunate loss of the above vessel, and the fate of the passengers; and as many of them have friends in this city, we publish the following particulars:- On the 14th August last, the Letitia anchored in the Bay of Porto Prago, to take in water and some fresh provisions, and on the 19th, although the weather is represented as being moderate, it appears she drifted on the rocks, and shortly after bilged and became a wreck. The passengers and crew were all landed safely, being near the shore…but little or nothing was saved of the cargo or the passengers' luggage."lxxxi*

The Grey family were safe on dry land as described in Humphrey's the letter to his cousin. They had lost all their possessions but luckily Humphrey had retained his money belt with sufficient funds to continue their journey.lxxxii

The next part of their adventure is well documented by Frank Murray on the in *My Early Pioneers and Their Families* Website and is a story worth reading. The British Consul soon managed to secure them a birth on the "Hesperus" from Cape Verde to Rio de Janiero, arriving in October 1828. The passenger list from the *Hesperus,* with Captain Allen, clearly shows all the Grey family members.

lxxxiii

There they waited several months for another ship, the Brig *Ann* for the final part of the voyage leaving Rio on the 7th March and arriving in Hobart on the 3rd June 1829 as shown in the passenger list.lxxxiv

> The following are the passengers per brig Anne,
> Captain Samuel Cornby, which arrived at this port,
> on the 3d instant, from Rio Janeiro, Captain and
> Mrs. Moriarty and three children, Mr. Mrs. and Miss
> Moore, and 3 children, Mr. Gray, Mr. Foster, Mr.
> Macnamara, Mr. Riley, Mr. and Mrs. Mc Ghie, and
> three children, Mrs. Clarke and Mrs. Huggard, all
> originally passengers per Letitia, from London,
> Captain Clements, late of the Colonial vessel Glory.
> Passengers from Rio—Mr. Malony, also John Ring,
> Matthew Mayes, Darby Cleary, John Cashman, Dan
> Heily, Patrick Murray, and John Leaky ; Labourers
> from Ireland who emigrated to Rio and being in dis-
> tress, were forwarded by the British Consul, to this
> port. The Letitia was wrecked on the 19th August,
> last, at St Jago, with 60 persons on board. They re-
> mained at St. Jago 8 days, the British Consul then
> hired an American vessel to take them to Rio, at
> which place they remained (with the exception of 11)
> 5 months, and the British Consul humanely paid for
> their lodging and diet, and chartered the Ann for this
> place for £900. The 11 of the passengers and crew,
> which remained at St. Jago, (by their own desire)
> all died of fever, and were buried in one spot. A
> fever broke out among the passengers between St.
> Jago and Rio, and 7 died.
> The passengers per Letitia, lost all their property,
> among which was £11,00 in specie, belonging to
> Mr. Gray, who has arrived with his family at this
> port.

As ever Humphrey, with his lifetime experience of supplying goods to the Army in his role at the Commissionariat and his astute eye for business opportunities, had imported 668 baskets of tobacco which would most certainly have helped restore the health of their financial losses.[lxxxv]

Their story was well publicised and almost immediately the survivors of the *Letitia* became prominent figures in the small community and also drew a great deal of sympathy from the local press;

> turing.
> We respectfully beg to suggest the opportunity that pre-
> sents itself to the Lieutenant Governor, to give these care-worn
> sufferers, who ventured across the great deep to settle on our
> coasts, suitable grants of land to encourage them, and in some
> measure to recompense them for their losses, free of all re-
> strictions, that they be enabled to write home to their friends,
> that their misfortunes have not been attended with utter ruin,
> or hopeless despair, and that they may write home to encou-
> rage other emigrants to come here from the kind reception they
> met.

Shorty after their arrival the Greys moved to Avoca to be with their cousins and other Irish-born, Protestant, families in the district. The land they chose, called Eastbourne, is shown in the 1837 map below, along with James Gray, near the river junction and two lots owned by William on the St Paul's River.

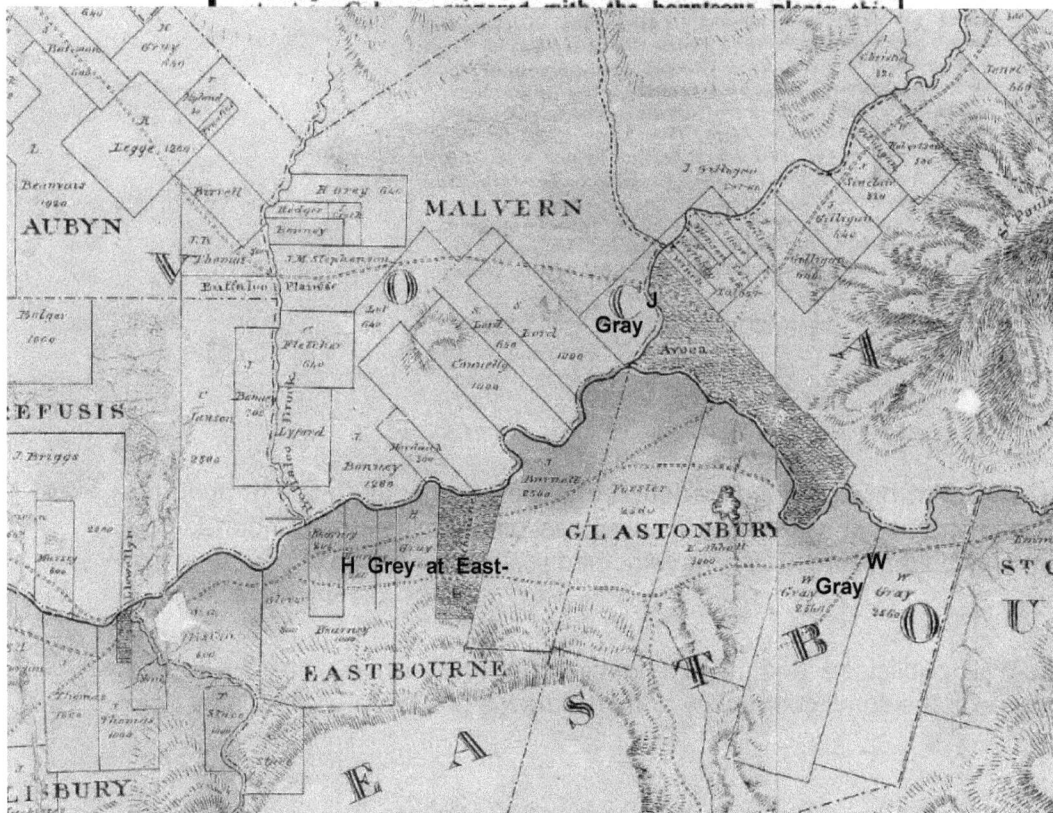

Once there the family began the task of building, first for protection and then for the pleasure of creating a home. However their most immediate concern was the real and perilous threat to the safety of the family. The Aborigines at the time were waging a fierce guerilla war against the invaders of their land. They had arrived at the height of the Black War and were situated on the frontier of the British Empire in the middle of the Northern Midlands Nation occupied by the Tyerrernotepanner (Stoney Creek people).

# BOX SEVEN: JOURNEY TO AVOCA, THE GRAY FAMILY

## Day of Arrival

Imagine, if you will, the theatre being played out at Hunter Island Dock in Hobart, Van Diemen's Land on the 20th August 1827. The Ship *Medway,* having anchored, is swarmed upon by activity; small boats everywhere, sails, ropes, shouts, men stowing, tying, winching, and unconstrained anticipation.

The *Medway*[lxxxviii] was a passenger ship with 35 paying customers, a far cry from the convict ships arriving regularly from England carrying around 2000 each year to a place regarded as a huge prison by both the British establishment and the Island's administrators. At this time there were just over 17,000 Europeans amongst whom were 7000 convicts. Incidentally there were also 300,000 sheep on the Island. The sight of free setters stepping ashore was still something of a novelty although becoming increasingly routine. By the time Humphrey Grey arrived in 1829 the population had risen by another 3000[lxxxix] and increased exponentially to well over 70,000 by the time the Island became known as Tasmania in 1856.

Once on dry land the passengers must have taken some time to gain their land legs. The family had been onboard the *Medway* for four months leaving London on the 1st April 1827 with only one stop at Bahia in Brazil. Ships plied a well-seasoned route from England, south west across the Atlantic to South America, which avoided the dreaded doldrums of the coast of West Africa. From there they went south east, below South Africa and collecting the trade winds, on to their destination. Trying to pull up before actually hitting land was some-what problematic, with hundreds of ships ending up on wild west coast shores with over 1000 known ship wrecks on the coast of Tasmania since European exploration began. Some of the wrecks are known about although many more ships were lost without trace. For those on board the *Medway* it would have been a particularly cold and wet voyage through the winter months in the Southern Ocean.

The passenger list reads like a Who's Who of colonial society, names which will reappear for generations to come and many of their descendants remain in Tasmania including; Archer, Connolly, Jennings, Wood, Bethune, Kemp, Mortimer, Meredith, Ross and Hopkins.

The focus here is on members of the Gray clan and it may be worth exploring each one's perspective and reactions to their new environment, beginning with Mrs Anne Gray. At 67 she was the Gray family matriarch. Born in 1760, Anne had married Richard Gray MD and lived in Birr, also known as Parsonstown, in King'sCounty for most, if not all, of her married life. She raised four sons; William, James, Basil and Richard. Her reasons for being there were in all probability a mix of practical necessity and sentiment. Her husband had died some time before and as a doctor in Ireland material fortune was doubtful. Being a widow in the early part of the 19th Century Anne would most certainly have been dependent on her children for her worldly comforts. Emotionally it is easy to understand her desire to be close to her children and an ever expanding brood of grandchildren. Her third son, Basil, had joined the Royal African Corps as an ensign and had died unmarried in Sierra Leone. Richard, her youngest, followed his father's footsteps and became a doctor. He lived at Nenagh in County Tipperary. So, for her, regardless of the stresses of her age, there really was little

## SHIPPING & COMMERCIAL INTELLIGENCE,
### Arrived at Hobart-Town,

Aug. 20.--The ship Medway, 450 tons, B. Wight, commander, from the Downs 1st of April, with a large assortment of merchandize, among which are 66 puncheons rum, 24 do. Geneva, 4 do. brandy, 30 hhds. vinegar, 155 casks wine, 7 cases Champaigne, 100 casks porter, 100 hhds. brown stout, 70 casks bottled do. 100 tons salt, 200 barrels Irish pork, 110 firkins butter, 26 do. lard, 24 large rolls Brazil tobacco, 600 deals, 10 crates crockery, 150 cases soap, 7 cases apothecary's stores, and a large quantity of plate, bar and hoop iron.

Passengers—Major and Mrs. Gray, (94th regt. infantry) Lieut. and Mrs. Gray, (8th regt. dragoon guards), Mrs. Gray, senior, 3 Masters and 1 Miss Gray, Mr. and Mrs. Levy and 4 children, Mr. and Mrs. Legge and 4 Misses Legge, Mr. Archer, (father of the Messrs. Archer of this colony), Mrs. Liscombe, Mr. Conolly, Mr. Jennings, Dr. Richardson, Messrs. Wood, Stacey and Reeve.

The Medway touched for refreshment at Bahia, and took on board at that port 5 tons of Brazil tobacco.

choice: poor and alone in Ireland or travelling with her two sons and their families to an Island about as far away as one can possibly be from home.

Major William Gray appears at the top of the list of passengers in the shipping news, which in a way reflects a little about his own sense of self and standing. At 33 he had spent most of his adult life as an Officer and resolute explorer of the wilds of West Africa. William was confident and self-assured and stepping ashore for him in a foreign land was a familiar and comfortable situation. This situation provided everything he could wish for. He was now a big fish in a very small pond. His military bearing and rank gave him easy access to the most influential members of the colony. The recent publication of his book *Travels in Western Africa in the years 1818,19,20 and 21 from the River Gambia, through Woolli, Bondoo, Galam Kasson, Kaarta and Foolidoo to the River Niger* would have given him some celebrity status in the Colony, which he undoubtedly relished. The fact that his expedition never actually set eyes on the River Niger and that by any measure it was a costly failure in both human life and resources could be conveniently overlooked in such a far-away place as VDL. Never let the truth get in the way of ambition.

In a Colony administered by Lt Colonel George Arthur along military lines, William knew well the rules, mores and hidden agendas associated with such a culture. Added to this only recently the Colony had become separated from NSW and now acted in its own right and answered directly to London, which gave Governor Arthur far greater powers and patronage. Everything fitted into place for William. His timing was perfect, land grants and allocation of convicts were still in the hands of the Governor which worked well in William's favour resulting in a 2,560 acre grant on the St Pauls River, Avoca.[xc] William was clearly in charge, He was a self-designated leader, a position he never doubted and taken for granted by the remainder of the family.

Beside William was his wife, Ellen whose full name was Elleanor Toler. She was the daughter of James and Ismenia Kingsley of Ballyhogan[xci]. Ellen and William had been married for nearly five years and already had three young children: Richard aged 3 and William Kingsley Gray, and Humphrey Arthur who was born either just before they left or perhaps on board.

The notion of 'Free Settler' is worth considering. While superficially it may seem to describe a homogeneous group of people the reality was often quite different. While they might not have been in prison ships, individuals, especially the women and children, were often severely constrained by gender, age and their destinies determined by others. As Kate Dougharty observed when referring to the families' decision to emigrate;

After many consultations, Humphrey, William and James came to a decision. They would not throw the burden of deciding on to their wives. That was a man's part.[xcii]

However they did have four female servants who probably also worked for the whole Gray clan. Nothing is known about their servants. Perhaps for them it was an opportunity for a new life away from the unending poverty and constrained life in Ireland and they were being paid! In a way they may have had marginally more of a choice in deciding their future than the Gray ladies. Their prospects for finding a suitable husband were encouraging, with far more men in the Colony to choose from and the opportunities of making a far richer live for themselves and their children than they ever would have had at home.

Lt James Gray and his wife Mary disembarked together[xciii]. James was bright, chatty and charming with a cheerful disposition. Always willing to help others and taking directions from his older, self-assured brother, he and Mary would hastily have settled somewhere on shore. Mary at 25 close to giving birth to her second child was most assuredly pleased to leave the *Medway*. Anna Frances Gray, known always as Fanny, was born three weeks later on the 13 Sept 1827.[xciv] The first of many Gray children to begin life in VDL. Their first child Blanche, the '1 Miss' listed in the Shipping News, was only a little over one year old when carried ashore on that day.[xcv]

Mary's maiden name was Legge and she was far from alone. On board were her brother Robert Vincent Legge[xcvi] and sisters Eliza, Sarah, Alicia & Frances while their eldest brother William Vincent had stayed behind in Ireland. All siblings later married.[xcvii] For Alicia at least it was a shipboard romance leading to an eventual marriage with Mr. Jennings, one of her fellow passengers.

The vista each of the travelers was met with was one of awe and wonder. Set below an imposing, eternal mountain, perhaps capped by grey cloud or even snow. Their eyes would be greeted by a small but resolute village.

This delightful picture by George Frankland portrays a often-played out scene of a family stepping ashore and feeling the texture and grit of dirt under their feet for the first time after months at sea at exactly the time of the Gray's arrival. Frankland the artist, had only just arrived in July with his wife and children to commence work as the Colony's Surveyor General. He led the department for ten years until his death in 1838. His profession demanded a meticulousness to detail so it seems unlikely he would have made up this family image. [xcviii]

Figure 6 Immigrants arriving at Hunter Island (now Hunter Street), Hobart Town Van Diemen's Land, by George Frankland

Does this picture depict the Gray clan? Franklin titles it immigrants arriving at Hunter Street. He had arrived only a few weeks earlier and not many immigrant ships were to anchor at the port However this remains speculation. The Grays arrived on the *Medway* with '3 masters and 1 Miss'. The picture shows a man holding a baby who may have been Humphrey Arthur Gray, son of William and Eleanor and the toddler Blanche Eliza b 1826 daughter of James and Mary.

The woman trying to step out of the boat is clearly struggling, much to the amusement of her servant, as she pushes her mistress with both hands. Mary was eight months pregnant at this time which would certainly inhibit her agility when exiting a dinghy onto a high-walled dock and might explain her testy temperament on this occasion, if indeed it is she. The man, obviously a gentleman, complete with top hat, may have been one of the Gray's and is most probably James, as it is hard to countenance the idea of Major William taking on such an indignity.

Once on land the family were to stand at Hunter Island, which had been the main hub of shipping since 1804. It was connected to land by an isthmus only crossable during low tide In earlier times, 'those who could not wade were duly shipped

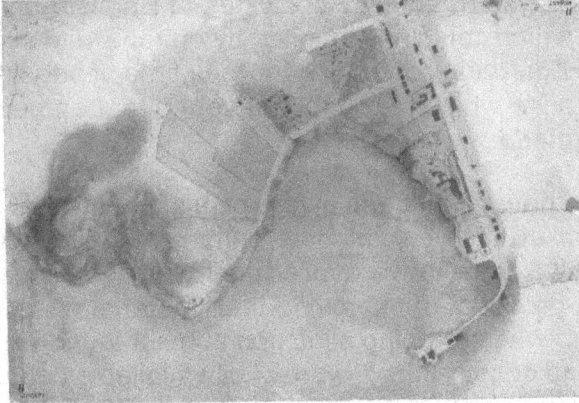

Figure 7 Hunter Street Wharf - Hobart  Tasmanian Archives

upon the backs of brawny, sailors, whilst the ladies were conveyed in sedan- chairs, made of the willing hands of two able seaman'.

However, as can be seen on the left in Frankland's picture, convict chain gangs were working on the causeway during this period in 1826 although by the time their cousin Humphrey Grey and his family arrived in 1829 it had been complete and described as a; *substantial causeway of masonry, wide enough for two carts to pass, and a good path for foot passengers.*[xcix]

### Social Intricacies

Looking beyond, Hobart was now just over 20 years old and a mix of well laid out streets set out by Macquarie a decade before and a growing collection of ramshackle buildings with ad hoc paths and byways. It was strong, growing and well established but still essentially a Military run prison with gangs of convicts, guards, people with a ticket of leave, police and British regiments. The legal system was harsh and uncompromising: public executions were regular events. Notice the casualness or black humour of the writer in January of 1827.

three shillings a bushel. The Judge opens the Court at Launceston. Twelve criminals executed on the gallows at Hobart Town, 17. 18. Heavy thunder showers. Government house long in a

There was also an increasing number of free settlers who by their very presence were beginning to redefine the Colony, its culture and character.

Not only that but there were individuals who were very much taking control of their own destiny despite the fact that they had arrived in a prison ship. Even though it mirrored the stifling class system and social divides of English society there were some clear differences which could be exploited by anyone with skills, talent or an eye for opportunities. For many convicts, after their time of servitude was over they were able to make a life which they could never have dreamed of had they remained in England or Ireland.

The Grays however may not have even been aware of this, they were very definitely in the privileged stratum of this very intimate community. They also seized opportunities of which would never have availed themselves in Ireland land, higher social status and the prospect of improving their material wealth. It was a good time to be in VDL. Land was still being allocated subject to individual funds where £1 bought one acre and convict labour was readily available coupled with a thriving economy illustrated well in the article 'Chronology of 1827 for Van Diemen's Land' from the Hobart Town Courier.[ci]

Extracts include;

*Jan*

*The ship Resolution from Calcutta to Valparaiso puts in for refreshment. 28. The Hope arrives with goods and passengers from London, and H.M.S Success with British silver. 31. Sails to explore Rottnest island the north-eastern coast of New Holland.*

*Feb*

*Imports at Hobart town for 1826, amount to £19183, imported in five ships. The exports to £14508. Only one puncheon of rum left in the bonded store. The Admiral Cockburn arrives from London with merchandize, and the Australian company's ship City of Edinburgh, from Leith. Mr. G. Barnard, surveys King's island. The interior of Van Dieman's land divided into five-police districts, and police magistrates appointed to each, viz, at New Norfolk, Oatlands, Campbell town, Norfolk plains, and Richmond. The American brigs General Sucre and Bolivar, arrive from Manilla, and the Caledonia with goods from London.*

*March*

*Commercial revenue collected at Hobart town during the year 1826, amounts to £23262. A Tasmanian agricultural company projected, with a capital of £10,000, to export the produce of the country. A memorial is proposed to the Home Government re-questing assistance in bringing free labourers. A chamber of commerce is also talked of; neither of these undertakings is yet carried into effect. The Marquis of Lansdown arrives with tea. 24. The Hugh Crawford sails for England with produce. Several new mercantile houses of respectability established in Hobart town.*

*May*

*The whole value of imports into Van Diemen's land during 1826, amounted to £100,000 the exports were double those of the former year, and amounted to about £50,000.*

*August*

*Sugar scarce at Hobart-town and sells at 9d. a lb. Fools-cap paper sold at £4. a ream*

*September*

*Bacon and hams very generally cured in Van Diemen's land, and malt liquor brewed.*

*October*

*Freight from London to Hobart-town from 4 to £5 a ton, a passenger £80. November*

*A new Bank, to be called the Derwent bank, capital £20,000, established to commence operations on the 1st of January. The old bank of Van Diemen's land changed into a joint stock company.*

The price of wheat rose from three to eight shillings during that year. The contrast between such optimism and vigor compared with their home country must have been manifest and most certainly encouraging.

## Family Matters

Mary and James had more pressing matters to deal with as the birth of their second daughter was imminent. Settling in to a new town, finding a place to stay and arranging for Mary's confinement. Luckily (or unluckily!) she had four sisters to help and maids in abundance. On the 13th September Anna Frances Gray was born. Although it did not take long for the couple to increase their family even more with the birth of James Vincent Gray on the 15th November 1828.[cii]

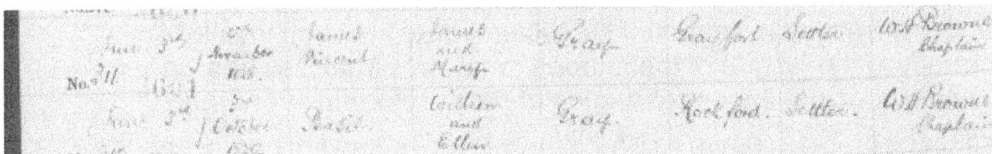

Willian and Ellen were not far behind with the birth of Basil on 3rd Oct 1829. James and Basil were both christened on the same day, 3rd June 1830 at St John's Church in Launceston, by Rev W Browne.

**Travelling to Avoca**

So far, the family had travelled from King's County in Ireland, sailed to England, probably to Bristol, over land to London and followed by months at sea to reach Hobart. Their journey was far from over. The roads through VDL at this time were little more than tracks, often muddy and impassable, with few bridges, although interspersed by small villages and resting places. These included Brighton, Crown Inn, Espie, Swan Inn, Green Ponds, and many more on their weeks journey.[ciii] Travellers had ample time to absorb a remarkable and mysterious landscape as they were jogged, bumped and shaken on the back of bullock drays most aptly described by Brett who in 1830 viewed the scenery as 'most romantic, and would repay the traveller for the fatigue of his journey'.[civ]

For Anne Gray, in her late-sixties, the romance may have been tempered by the fragilities of age and the unforgiving nature of such conveyances. She would have empathised with Mrs Augustus Prinsep's experience in her trip from Hobart to Launceston in March 1829:

Figure 8 St John's Church 1825

I shall pass over the constant repetition of stony roads and steep hills, telling you, once for all that except in the centre of the island, in the neighborhood of the salt marshes the whole surface is undulated with ridges of rocky hills, beautiful indeed, to the traveler in search of the picturesque; but to an invalid like myself, adding greatly to the fatigue of the journey (and) my bones still bear testimony to the inconvenience of the sharp angles of hard rocks which protrude in the newly formed roads of Van Diemen's Land.[cv] For Mary Gray with a baby only a few weeks old her journey may have mirrored that of Louisa Anne Meredith on her first trip to Swansea.

The road became quite colonial, that is, execrably bad, and the scenery too monotonous to divert my attention for a moment from the misery of the rough jolting we suffered, and form the cares lest every shock should disturb or hurt my baby, whom I dared not trust in the maid's arms for fear she might drop him out whilst saving herself from on of the incessant jolts, which threatened fractures and dislocations at every step.[cvi]

The Gray party would have been quite a spectacle. Loaded with all the supplies, equipment and material needed to establish a European home on land they had not seen. Nor would they have much knowledge about the nature of the soil, flora and fauna. They also needed guns and ammunition for protection from the elements, natives and bushrangers. The group consisted of William Gray and his wife Ellen with four year old Richard, William around two and baby Humphrey, also James Gray and Mary with toddler Blanche and newly born Anna Frances.

Mary's sisters stayed in Hobart while their brother Robert Legge quite possibly joined the expedition as far as Avoca. He went a few miles farther east just before Fingal and took up land at Cullenswood. Also accompanying them were an assembly of their four servants, assigned convicts and bullock drivers and an assortment of other folk. A week or two after leaving Hobart the families were able to finally stop and firmly plant their mark on land which had been allocated them. William named their property Rockford after Ellen's family home in Ireland located on St Paul's River while James settled at a beautiful site on the South Esk River for Grayfort.

Figure 9  Grayfort 1895

# BOX EIGHT: HOUSES AS A REFLECTION OF CHARACTER

Figure 10 Grayfort photo by Annie Rushton 2015

The decision to emigrate was not only a result of external events but the disposition of the people involved. Looking at the houses it is easy to see how the character of each man is reflected in the houses they designed and built. The houses are intriguing. It is rare to have anything left from that time but to be able to relate and match each one to the people who created them is even more fascinating.

Taking into account the nature of the men and times, it is reasonable to assume the women had little say such matters. The houses are: Grayfort and Rockford constructed by brothers James and William in the late 1820s. Eastbourne House build by Humphrey in about 1832. Grayfort shows some imagination and inventiveness in the use of natural stones seemingly collected from the site which its comfortably with Lt James Gray's disposition.[cvii] James had little money and living in the shadow of his brother seems likely to have been a pleasant, likeable individual, although woefully impractical. What he lacked in the ability to plan ahead and hard work, he made up for in flamboyancy and show. He was not averse to being called Captain Gray, rather than Lieutenant on occasions, and it would seem his desire to dress well was one factor which eventually led to financial anxiety. As a result, his material affairs were not overly successful. Rockford

The house that William built was solid, austere, and military and positioned in a commanding position over the valley. It was a statement of ownership, authority and control. It even looks over the family graveyard as a way of paternal protectiveness. He was a confident, self-important and pompous character as Margaret so poignantly observed in Dougharty's book;

*She had more than once been Cousin William's audience, and had failed to get a word in edgeways. Much as she liked him, this could be very trying.* [cviii]

Figure 11 Rockford Photo by Annie Rushton

William Gray's house was the centre of political and administrative influence in the district, where he took on the role of both magistrate and special constable. He also hosted the visit of two governors at different times: Arthur[cix] in 1833 and Franklin 1839.[cx]

The story of Governor Arthur's stay is delightfully portrayed by Kate Dougharty later in this book, when she relays a tantalizing letter from William to Cousin Humphrey Grey.*Mrs. Grey wishes me to ask if you and Kitty would allow Catherine to visit us for a few days. We are expecting a visit from Governor and Suite, in two days' time.They wish to make a survey of the district.*[cx]

ATRICA.—The Lieutenant Governor visited Avoca on Saturday last, in the course of his tour through the colony. He was received at the residences of Mr Talbot, of Major and Captain Gray, and spent between two and three days in the District. On Saturday, His Excellency

AVOCA. — The Lieutenant Governor visited Avoca on Saturday last, in the course of his tour through the Colony he was received at the residences of Mr Talbot, of Major and Captain Gray, and spent between two and three days in the District. Tasmanian, April 12

Governor Sir John Franklin visited the district in 1839 and attended both the Gray brothers. Interestingly James rank appears to have risen to a captaincy for the occasion. cxii

The men were renowned explorers, Franklin in the Arctic and Gray in Africa. For those listening, their conversation must have been enthralling filled with tales of myth and marvel. Their stories of adventure and daring were part of the mythology of the times and had been reported by the Hobart Town Gazette and Southern Reporter in1819,

AFRICA.—Another enterprize to explore the termination of the Niger is undertaken, and, as in all former ones, with sanguine hopes of success. Captain Gray, of the Royal African Corps, is intrusted with the immediate charge of the expedition. He is represented as every way qualified for solving this geographical enigma; he has been seven years in Africa, and is well acquainted with the Jaloff language. The route is to be that of the Gambia river, which he had already entered. By letters which have    cxiii

William Gray's drive and determination is evident in his house which is a symbol of success. In 1828 he applied to have 1500 acres of Crown Land he was renting granted to him. The improvements, he claimed, included having cleared 50 acres, and the running of 360 cattle, 1700 sheep and 5 horses. He had built a £600 brick house, three and a half miles of fencing, outbuildings, stockyard and gardens. Arthur was so impressed with Gray's energetic approach that he increased the Land Board's recommendation to 2560 acres. cxiv

He even built a mill on his land at St Paul's Plain, the remnants of which are still present today.

William's character is also revealed through his role as a non-stipendiary magistrate and Chief District Constable. He had a fearsome reputation and 'dispensed tough sentences to local convict servants from the court that was held at his home. Sentences of flogging and chain ganging were common punishments from Gray.'[cxv] He was also severe when it came to disciplining his own servants and convicts working at Rockford as shown by Eliza's fate;

Major Gray charged Eliza Orrell with being absent all night. She was returned to second class at the House of Correction and was reassigned.[cxvi]

His enterprise and energy created the wealth and status he so craved and after a decade, he even declined an offer of £20,000 for Rockford. Which in hindsight was a mistake. Soon after the Colony succumbed to a severe depression, greatly devaluing the property.

Figure 78 Eastbourne by Richard Chuck 2017

Humphrey Grey's house on the other hand is a softer, com    posed  house clearly reflecting status and wealth but in a low key, understated manner. It is indeed a gentleman's residence which, by all accounts, is how he was seen by those who knew him well. The home exuded a warmth which was inviting and welcoming to anyone who crossed the doorstep. Inside it is well-lit, has a wide hallway and large rooms, even upstairs in the servants' quarters. It is well considered, planned and a family home which is a worthy reflection of Humphrey's disposition and values. He thought things through, made sure he had the necessary means to achieve his goals, and then acted.

This was exactly what he did when deciding to migrate. He allowed his cousins to go first, send back more information and carefully considered the options before making a clear decision. Once made, he determinedly set about its implementation. Eastbourne present and past

# Original Homestead

# Eastbourne after the fire

Figure 12 Eastbourne 2017 photo by
Annie Rushton

Old photos of Eastbourne curtesy of
Frank   O'Connor

**Manalargenna**

by Jules Dumont d'Urville

circa 1840

**Author's Note:**

Writing history is always problematic when delving into past happenings which still have resonance and meaning to individuals and communities living today. It is even harder when the author is one of those people. In this case the question was how best to examine the conflict which occurred between the Aboriginal people living in the area and the new English settlers, in this case the Gray family at Avoca.

There were several options: Leave it out of the book, acknowledge the prior ownership of the Northern Midland Nation peoples or attempt to discover and explain the differing perceptions from the diverse groups involved in the ensuring struggle. Disregarding the topic was not an acceptable solution, it would have simply compounded the ignorance of both past and present.

A statement acknowledging prior ownership was considered but rejected as too shallow once the research began to unravel the very real involvement the family had in the war.

The outline below is flawed and does not do justice to either side. It is however a modest attempt to reveal some of the different perspectives and tangled truths associated with the many facets of the unresolvable conflicts of the 1820s and 30s in the remote Fingal Valley of Van Diemen's land.

While it may offend there is no intention to do so. The aim is to share and learn together about our mutual past no matter how confronting and perplexing that may be. It is hoped the reader will approach the story with an open and receptive attitude.

When reading this section it may be prudent to keep in mind the well-known adage,

*'History is written by the Victors.' Churchill*

## The Tyerrernotepanner Man

Rockford at dusk, the year 1830. A hunting party led by Major Gray stealthily works its way through the forest in search of prey. Animals are in abundance, bandicoots, wallabies, kangaroo, the occasional emu and perhaps a tiger. Tonight they are safe. Gray and his men are in pursuit of human quarry, the natives who live on his land. The Governor has ordered that natives should wherever possible be captured rather than killed. Gray is a military man and follows orders. They spot their targets, give chase and fail. The eventful evening was shared far and wide and even reported in the local newspaper;

A party, under Major Grey, went out in pursuit: overtook a few blacks; one was seized; but he was so smeared with grease, that he slipped through the hands of his captors.[cxvii]

The focus of this section is, however, not on Gray and his hunters but on the person who was 'seized'. Who was he? What is known about him, his family, thoughts, life and culture? What was he wearing, why was he smeared with grease? What did he eat, why and how can he be understood as a person dealing with the terrible events now engulfing his world?

In reality, this can never be known but there are some pieces of evidence from history which can provide just a glimmer, a minute insight into his world, his past and his life. Using this it may be possible to bring together the pieces of the puzzle but in the end it will, sadly, remain one with many bits missing and large gaps in the final picture. To give this man a name, an identity, would in a way deny who he was, it would be like making up a name for the Unknown Soldier, and it would simply be a contrivance. He is in effect a symbol of his race.

Clearly it must have been a terrifying moment to be assaulted and 'seized' by a white hunter. The hunters smell, clothing, breath and weapons would all have been frightening and foreign. If caught the native would have been killed or worse still captured, wrenched from his land and people and eventually have died both in spirit and flesh. Why would he have been so scared? At this time many of his family and clan members had been killed by the white settlers. Among these may well have been his wife, mother, children grandparents or indeed members of another clan or perhaps the neighbouring plangermairreenner people from the east side of Mt Ben Lomond, or Turbuna.

The plangermairreenner were, like other clans on his boundary, the plindermairheremener and the tonenerweenerlarmenne, all part of a 'federation' of the north-east clans. This ensured the clans access the hinterland, and the land-locked clans to access the coast. The meenamatta country, that is the land running from Turbuna (along the Esk River) to the Blue Tiers/St Helens area is likely to have been used much like the commons in England, and was a hunting ground between the ridges running east-west.[cxviii]

*Regardless of the political, military and social events swirling around him the primary concern for his family was to protect their children.*

It is safe to assume he knew the settlers by now, if not by name certainly by reputation. He had learned some English although few white men could understand his language. One called Batman was well known to the Aborigines in the area, especially to the Ben Lomond Nation. He and his roving group of hunters were known to surround sleeping families, shoot and kill as many men, women and children as they could and then to steal their children. On one occasion he and his men killed fifteen and he executed two more, he said to put them out of their misery.[cxix] The white people also had an army regiment close by and police and many others who were only too willing to     fight and kill his people. He would have heard of their Chief called Arthur who wore black, the colour of his own skin and who carried  a small  black  book: a colour soon  to  become synonymous with death. Arthur was leading  the war and many years later it would be known by some of his community as Arthur's War.[cxx]

He would, of course, have known many more terrible events at the time. He was liter-ally engaged in a fight not only for his own life but for his whole Nation and their land, Lutrawita.[cxxi]

The reason for the war he knew was simple: the white men wanted his tribal lands. This was not always so. Just a few seasons earlier it was doubtful he had ever seen a white man or even known of their existence. He would have grown up living with his family group including his parents who were probably married in their teens and stayed together for life. His brothers and sisters, grandparents and other relatives all would have lived together, eat-ing, telling stories, sharing, fighting and laughing just as any other group of humans have done for ever - making babies, giving birth, caring for their sick and elderly and making their homes warm and comforting.

He wore Kangaroo skins and smeared his body with wallaby fat for warmth.  His  body held deep scars, possibly from scarification at puberty. The marks  may also have indicated which clan he was from and were very pronounced and easy to identify.[cxxii] He  and  his family  slept  in  bark  huts  build  for warmth and protection depending on the season. In fact they lived by the seasons which determined where they hunted, the area they would move to  and indeed their social interaction with people from other Nations to find marriage  part-ners.  There were strict social conventions related to marriage  and punishments for adultery, unsuitable marriages and for any other infringements  of  tribal laws.

As with many human societies, tasks and duties were often gender defined. For example women made necklaces, reed baskets, collected berries or caught possums and wombats while men used wooden spears and waddies with incredible skill and accuracy. Families in any society need the companionship of others for a whole range of reasons including finding a partner, mutual benefits from hunting and protection against hostility. He and his family were also part of a Clan, that is 'a group of people who called them-selves  by  a  particular  name  and  were  known  by  that  or  other  names  to  other people'.[cxxiii] This man's family may have been from one of five Clans who lived in and around the area of Avoca although we only know the name of three: Leterremairrener (Port Dalrymple) at East Tamar, Panninher (Norfolk Plains)  and  the  Tyerrernotepanner (Stoney Creek  people)  at  Campbell  Town. [cxxiv]It could be assumed that he was part of the latter group which lived the closest to the encounter with Gray. Of course, we will never know but for the purposes of this story it is helpful to try and picture the people living in the area.

Their Clan had a leader or 'chief', older, well regarded for his fighting and physical skills, intelligence and ability to lead. His Clan was made up of family groups related to him or associated in some way. Moulteheerlargenna, also known as Eumarrah, was the leader of the Leterremairrener clan whom he would also have known. Eumarrah was well known to George Augustus Robinson, the notional Protector of Aborigines and certainly tried at first to come to some resolution with the white settlers. cxxv

Some of his friends and clan people were Memerlannelargenna, Ningernooputenner, possibly Pleengkotetenner. He may also have known people from neighbouring clans in his Nation such as Plerperoparner from the Leterremairrener.cxxvi The women he knew or was related to usually joined their husband's clan and vice versa, although this was not always the case if there was a quarrel.cxxvii

Finally Clans found that there was strength in numbers with several forming into

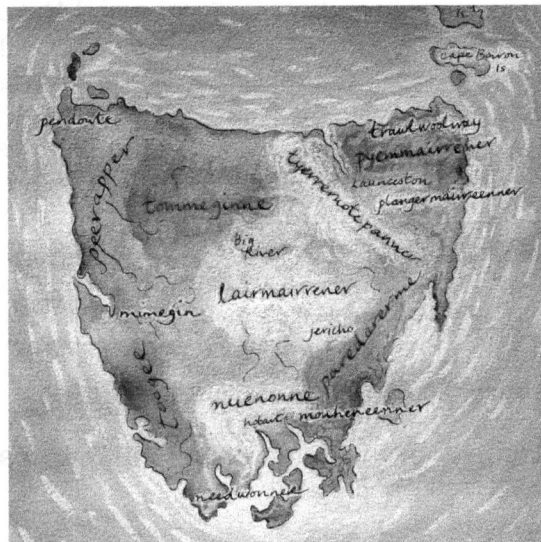

Figure 13 Tribal boundaries of the Tasmanian Aboriginal people, map, Jessie Ginsborg-Newling 2008

a Nation. Although there were nine nations in VDL this man may only have been aware of those closet to his Clan. That is the Ben Lomond Nation north of the South Esk River, the north-west corner of the Oyster Bay Nation and perhaps the Big River Nation. His was called the North Midlands Nation with an original population estimated to be between 300 and 400 although it may have been much higher. According to Ryan the settlers killed at least 300 outright between 1820 – 30.cxxviii

His Nation lived in their territory and were bound by obvious land marks such as rivers, mountain ranges etc. The clan boundaries can be easily understood by studying the topography of Tasmania. Clans and Nations also had control of the richness of their land in his case the open, dry plains and eucalyptus woodlands with an abundance of Kangaroo and other animals.

The Clan used fire (made with wood rubbing or stones) to manage the land. They knew that after the ash had settled new growth would appear quickly and their animals would come hopping back, allowing them to take only what they needed. The men were proficient spear throwers and could strike down a moving animal or human from long distances with ease. How peculiar it must have seemed to see white people killing their Kangaroo only to leave the carcasses to rot while building fences to keep in strange animals which needed so many people to look after them, and for one person to have much more than they needed. At times during certain seasons other Nations were allowed to also take the animals they needed while his Clan was permitted to move through theirs for different food and important things such as red ochre, with trade routes to the East Coast and the Mountains of the Big River Tribe.

There were of course disputes and fighting between clans and Nations, over territory, women and all the age old causes of dispute between humans. As with any Nation of people they held complex spiritual beliefs about the World. It would, however, be presumptuous and disrespectful to even try to discuss such matters in this context. He and his people knew that they had lived on the land for thousands of years and that they had arrived by land and the sea had risen to leave them on Trouwunna. They were also acutely aware that their world was now being torn apart and would never be the same.

There was far more to this man's life than a few lines such as these can ever hope to offer. Nor is it nearly enough to pay tribute to him and his people but will hopefully engender some humanity and just a little compassion into this story.[cxxix]

However while most of his life may have been created from my imagination Jim Everett is real and this is his story. My family and country.

### Jim Everett-puralia meenamatta

Based on the eastern side of Turbuna (Mt Ben Lomond) is Plangermiarreenner Country, my clan family beginning from my main ancestor's matriarchal line. Wapperty was a daughter of Manalargenna, originally from a north Oyster Bay clan, the Leetermairremener. Manalargenna married a Plangermairreenner woman, no name recorded, and had three daughters to her, Wottecowidyer, Wyalooberer, and Wapperty, my traditional grandmother. Manalargenna's first wife died and he later married Tanleboneyer, a much younger woman who was known as a warrior in the fight against the occupiers of their land. They had no children from their marriage.

Manalargenna had fought the British during the Black War and eventually accepted George Robinsons terms to travel to Flinders Island. Reaching shore he realised he had been deceived by Robinson. Manalargenna shaved his head as a mark of deep personal shame before stepping ashore.

Wapperty married a Maori named Miti, son of Te Pahi, a chief of the Bay of Islands at Aotearoa (NZ). Miti was accompanying Te Pahi as they travelled on a trading ship to Sydney to visit Governor King to drum up trade for his tribe. Their stay on Cape Barren Island was short and her relationship with Miti and was, one must assume, a quick fling. Wapperty later gave birth to Elizabeth, nick named Betsy, who married James Everett, a sealer working the islands. They had three children, Robert, Gertrude, and James.

James married Florence Williams (nee Dobson) an English woman who had been born at Horton, Tasmania in 1877. Florence married twice, firstly Richard Maynard who died, and then James Everett, Betsy and James Everett's son. He was my grandfather on my father's side. Florence and James had six children, 3 boys and 3 girls, my father being the third born. Three children were born, my brother Eric, and my sister Barbara, all deceased. I was the second born, and our mother lost a boy at birth between Eric and me. My mother, Ena Gwendoline Maynard, has her family line go back to Wottecowidyer and Wyalooberer, Wapperty's sisters. My mother's family line details are somewhat complex due to broken strands in historical records and is similar to my father's family line.

*Figure 1 Tanleboneyer courtesy of UTAS*

*Figure 1 Wapperty, 70 years old [picture] / J. W. Beattie NLA*

Wapperty at age 70, Tasmania, Her two older sisters were , Wottecowidyer and Wyalooberer.This is my family, a big extended family with many links to other families through our past history from the ending of hostilities [Black War] until this very day. I grew up with my grandparents on my mother's side, my father's parents had gone long before a time my memory can recall. Like most Aborigines my life has been to grow up understanding that we are still colonised, and that there is no such thing as 'post- colonialism'. My grandfather, Edgar Maynard, was born on Cape Barren Island, and lived with my family on neighbouring Flinders Island where he died in 1968. He told me his stories of being coerced through the general class-conscious island society, and when he travelled as a seaman around Tasmania and placed in a category of being of an inferior race.

My parents told me similar stories of being conditioned to accept that they were not white, and not black, they were no-one. Out of my immediate family it was I only who decided things needed to change, and joined the Aboriginal political movement already established in Tasmania. During this period I knew that it would be necessary that I connect with Meenamatta Country, to camp around the regions of our clan and the other clans in the area. I had grown up being told that we didn't exist, that all Tasmanian Aborigines had been killed out by 1876 when Truginini died. By the time I was 30 years of age, I had pursued more study into my family history. Remember that what we had been conditioned to believe was blatantly untrue, and designed to affirm the government decision that there were no more blacks left in Tasmania. For me it was a challenge, and I dug deeper to know more of who I am, my Aboriginal identity, my clan country, and to de-code the lies to find the truth.

I have now camped many times on my clan country, my two eldest sons have camped there with me, or at other times, and have grown up to know who they really are through connection with country. They have both been Aboriginal Heritage Officers, and carry knowledge about our culture and our tools, camps, hunting and fire techniques, and most of all, how we are country as it is us.

See Appendix D for The Everett Family Tree

## On the road with Buck

One day I was drivin' with Buck Brown along the coast
An' we was talkin' about white coes on our land
'til the talk got real intense an' I wouldn't wanna boast
but we worked it all out from the start right to the end

Now it's easy enough to see, well it is to you an' me
why white fellas do their thing wrong way 'round
their Old Men made a structure with god being
He so that men had all the power on the ground

then they made their people's minds fit the Christian mould
an' they made a lot've boats to sail the seas
so they set to sail the seas in search of land an' gold
to plunder other lands an' never pay the fees

so they did an' found the gold, an' took our lands on the way
for that's the evil sort've system we now know
an' they came with hungry death an' blooded silver as their pay to rape our Mother for a new nation to build an' grow

an' they took our tribal land rights 'cause they said we wasn't here
an' the land grab was a killing thing with us against the flow
'til they beat us an' confined us and filled us full of fear
with a story of terra nullius we was crippled with nowhere else t' go

it's a lie we know for sure in it's christian sort've thing
'an they educate themselves in the lies the priest has told
but they believe it as a glory from the spirit of their king
for his power is protected by the lies that came from Old

now it's easy enough to see, well it is to you an' me
that the Old Men's system has bled them dry
as we look they embrace it 'cause it's strong for them t' be
an' it gives them power over land they make to die

for the lie they still ignore is our terror with a price
a terra nullius sort've thing that can't see black
for their embrace holds them tight, as if it were a vise
an' they believe it's the only way to hold us back

for the thing that holds their thinking is a system made by them
like a bottle full of history an' a story full've mud
for it hides their crimes against us too be sure we can't condemn
their values of indulgence an' the money smeared with blood

an' it holds them to a cost beyond their minds of what they do
with endless rape of our Great Mother an' the plunder of our lands
so yuh see Bro they still educate they're right in what they do
while they defend themselves against our cries an' our demands

an' they're taking a lot've our Mob with 'em as they climb their ivory tower
'til together they're like waves scrambling madly on the shoals
while we watch them jump an' tumble for white money an' its power
for this power gives 'em status while the whitey's own their souls

so there it is Ole Coe 'an we know their greed wont do 'em good
for our Great Mother will take control in a sorry end
so we do what we do until our Spirits are understood
for there's no way we're joining this mob 'round the bend

we got a job that aint got space for the way these fellas head
it's a picture don't yuh reckon, with a sad and bitter show
an' the devil these fellas pray to will come to claim the dead
but our Great Mother is the power that'll take 'em when they go.

Yeah Bro, it's easy enough to see, well it is to you an' me
Why white fellas do their thing wrong way 'round
But when their devil goes a running they'll really come t' see
The final price will be their end an' no tears from us will flow.

So take heed ole coe that we do our thing in a strong an' pure way
An' we always live with the way She has made for us to grow
An' hold no sorrow an' shed no tears for the way they end their day

'cause we told 'em for two hundred years, but they didn't wanna know.

jim everett     February 2000



Jim Everett was born on Flinders Island in 1942, Jim Everett left primary school at 14 to start work. His diverse lifestyle includes fifteen years at sea, three years in     the Australian Army,   and  fifty  years  formal  involvement  in  the  Aboriginal  Struggle.  His written works include plays, political papers and short stories, and writings published in ten major anthologies. Jim's other work includes television documentary and theatre produc-tion. He now lives on Cape Barren Island, often working away from home with various cultural arts programs including developing projects with Aboriginal community artists, as a Writer-in-Residence in Albany WA (2015), and in Wollongong (2015), and finishing a novel for  editing.  Most  recently  Jim  has  initiated  the  *We're Here*  project  in  collaboration with Contemporary Art Tasmania, exhibited in Salamanca Arts Centre's 2017 major exhi-bition *Proof of Life*, joined the Board of GASP!, and was an associate producer on the *Nightingale* film production.

**Protecting the Family**

*Regardless of the political, military and social events swirling around them the primary concern for the family was to protect their children.* This is highlighted in Katie's book when she refers to their mother's anguish for her children and very real fear from attacks by Aborigines. Fears for her precious children should they run into Aborigines, bushrangers or snakes filled her mind with daily tremors

It was not considered safe to allow young girls to ride unattended, they might

*Launceston, July* 14.—The four bushrangers who have committed the late robberies at Major M'Leod's, Mrs. Youl's, and Mr Comey's, I have much pleasure to inform you, are all taken and lodged in the gaol here. They were surprised in a hut on Captain Barclay's farm, near Gibson's ford,

hut on Captain Barclay's farm, near Gibson's ford, on the South Esk, by Mr. David Gray, Mr. W. Nairn Gray, Lieutenant James Gray, and Mr. James Attkin, accompanied by some assigned servants. The dogs on their approach gave the alarm, upon which Moulds, Gibson and Baker rushed from the hut, and Moulds fired at Mr. James Gray, but missed him. The fire was returned, and the robbers immediately fled, pursued by Lieut. Gray, Mr. W. Gray, and some assigned servants. The gentlemen being on horseback were thrown out by the intervention of a fence, and the fugitives were lost sight of. In the mean time a messenger had been

meet Aborigines, rough men, convicts in charge of soldiers, or even bushrangers, so an armed groom always rode near them.[cxxx]

They faced danger on two fronts: the lawlessness of their own people and the war between the Aboriginal Nations and Great Britain. The reality of the former became apparent when a few months after arriving they experienced their first known encounter with bushrangers which was reported as far away as Sydney in *The Australian* of 1828.[cxxxi]

Attacks by Bushrangers remained a constant and ongoing threat for most of their time in Avoca and certainly remained so until the 1850s. Early on the Black War intensified and become both treacherous and with fatalities occurring on both sides. In February nine natives were killed and three taken at St Paul's River.[cxxxii] Over the coming months retaliation and reprisals became melded into the insanity which is fashioned by war. In April 1829 two of Major Gray's shepherd's were speared killing Moses Garcia as reported in the

> *More atrocities by the Aborigines*
> –
>
> On Saturday week a party of Blacks came down upon a hut belonging to Major Gray E.I.C. s, near St Paul's Plains and speared two men one named Moses Garcia, the name of the other is at present unknown; one had received 9 spears in his back besides other wounds…

*Launceston Advertiser.*[cxxxiii]

James Gray's shepherd was also speared in December 1829 and another shepherd the following year. His property was subsequently attacked in September 1830 and again in May 1831. Other attacks at this time were noted by Batman in a letter to the Governor, August 29th

That there was some justification for the colonial terror, and some need for armed parties to restrain attack, where enable to make peaceable terms, a letter of Mr. Batman's may afford evidence. It was written officially from Ben Lomond, and says: " I have just time to say that the Natives last Thursday week murdered two men at Oyster Bay, and the next day they beat a sawyer about to death. On Sunday after they murdered a soldier. On last Wednesday they attacked the house of Mr Boultby, when he was absent ; and if it had not been for a soldier who happened to be there, they would have murdered Mrs. Boultby and all the children. On Friday last they murdered three men at a     hut belonging to Major Gray, and left a fourth for dead.[cxxxiv]

Understandably their precautions for protection always included arms to ward off attacks from either party. Captain Gray, of Avoca, was often seen standing over his threshold with a loaded musket. Men regularly took out their guns with them when they went to plough, sticking the weapon against some stump in the field. [Cxxxv]

### Gray Family Perspective

The Gray family were secure in the prevailing values and beliefs of their time. The British Government had claimed the Island under accepted European laws and conventions and it was their right to use the land as they pleased. They were British and subject to the laws, privileges and responsibilities which that entailed. When they stepped ashore in VDL, to them, it would have been akin to walking in Hyde Park in London. It was British soil. It was theirs and supported by the Law of the Land;

*The Australian Courts Act 1828 (Imp) s 24.* Thus British law was applied in the colony from the first. But problems regarding its application led in 1828 to the passing of the Australian Courts Act, s 24 of which provided that:

... all laws and statutes in force within the Realm of England at the time of passing of this Act ... shall be applied in the administration of justice in the Courts of New South Wales and Van Diemen's Land respectively, so far as the same can be applied within the said colonies ...[cxxxvi]

It is easy to see how Major Gray particularly would have felt at ease with such a notion. Below is an extract from his own book clearly expressing a set

viii        PREFACE.

remained of redeeming their fate by more successful exertions. Greece and Rome alternately fought and conquered, and were subdued by arms, the short summary of most nations' history, while it remained for the British Government alone to extend their empire through the enlightened agency of moral sway, of civil institutes, and Christian regulations, and convey to the hapless, the neglected, and the enslaved, the highest blessings which can dignify, improve, or adorn man.

Warmed with those feelings, I felt an honourable pride in being entrusted with a command to explore the uncultivated regions of Western Africa. It was a task of peril, but the measure of danger was the measure of honour; and with a strong distrust of my own capacity I accepted the office of conducting the expedition. As soon as I became acquainted with its objects, it may be naturally supposed that I felt some uneasiness; but such were the measures taken by a superior commander, *now no more,* that any insufficiency on my part was compensated by the wisdom of a gallant and enlightened officer. The objects of the mission were not the mere acquisition of territory, or the unfair advantage of commerce; they were the improvement of science, the enlargement of trade, and the consequent diffusion of increased happiness to the

PREFACE.        ix

African population. The sceptic in religion, and the would-be renovator of politics, may think differently on this subject; but every rational individual must feel that British life, British talent, and British treasure, would not be employed in such a quarter if there were not every wish to benefit and improve the condition of our degraded fellow creatures.

of mores and steadfastly held views related to his expeditions in Western Africa.[cxxxvii] It makes for interesting reading and highlights some ideas and words which were effortlessly transferable to his new setting. In it he mentions the term 'uncultivated'. This was critical to the thinking of Europeans at the time and provided justification for 'settling' uncultivated lands such as

## Litruwita or Van Diemen's Land

The general principles for the introduction of English law into a 'settled' as distinct from a 'conquered' colony were laid down by Blackstone in 1765. Justice Blackburn in *Milirrpum's* case put the distinction thus:

There is a distinction between settled colonies, where the land, being desert and uncultivated, is claimed by right of occupancy, and conquered or ceded colonies. The words 'desert and uncultivated' are Blackstone's own; they have always been taken to include territory in which live uncivilized inhabitants in a primitive state of society. The difference between the laws of the two kinds of colony is that in those of the former kind all the English laws which are applicable to the colony are immediately in force there upon its foundation. In those of the latter kind, the colony already having law of its own, that law remains in force until altered.[cxxxviii]

Similar views were also adhered to by the broader Gray family living in diverse parts of the British Empire as relayed in the criss-cross letter in Katie's book, written at the time to Humphrey by his younger brother Richard a Lieutenant in the 1st Ceylon Regiment. Richard and Major William would have little disagreement with each other. The British were at the same time in the process of brutally subduing the Vedda a minority group in Ceylon which Richard refers to in his letter.

The Veddas 'are the indigenous people of Sri Lanka with a culture dating back thousands of years."Sri Lanka's indigenous inhabitants, the Veddas 0r Wanniya-laeto ("forest-dwellers') as they call themselves – preserve a direct line of descent from the island's original Neolthic community dating from at least 16,000 and probably far earlier according to current scientific opinion.'[cxxxix]

Consequently upon arrival the Gray's were granted prime land, traditionally belonging to the Aboriginal 'North Midlands Nation' and so their battles began.


## The Family's War

It is important as far as possible to remain dispassionate when it comes to challenging and confronting issues such as 'Arthur's War' or the 'Black Wars' during the 1820s and 30s. This is almost an impossible task. The approach taken in this section is, therefore, to include the following documented records in chronological order related specifically to the Gray family and Avoca, leaving interpretation entirely for the reader.

Major William Gray was far from a passive observer during these turbulent times. He was the District Magistrate and Special Constable and represented the authority of the state. Batman most certainly referred to him frequently for advice and direction and in turn Gray provided Batman recognition and backing. Batman quoted

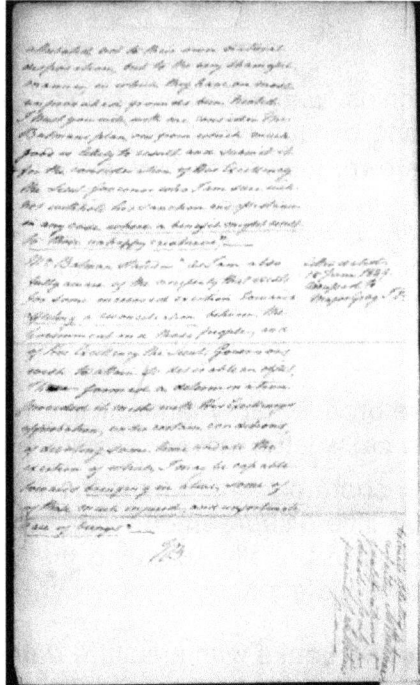

Gray in the letter below, indicating a high level of regard for his abilities in dealing with the current conflict. It is interesting to note that Batman was born in NSW and considered himself a native.

*Letter dated 15th June 1829 addressed to*

*J. Simpson Esq J.P.] Major Gray states - "I have just received the enclosed paper from Mr. J. Batman [indecipherable] whom, I am convinced, there is not any person in this part of the Country, more likely to succeed in the object he proposes, or who from his sentiments on the subject of the unwarranted, and brutal manner in which the system of retaliation now pursued by those wretched beings, was on most occasions called forth, is better suited to an enterprize which has for its end the amelioration of their circumstances, and*

*the prevention by capture of any wanton and useless loss of life, amongst a race of beings whose misfortune it is to be so ignorant of the blessings of civilized Society, and whose present hostile actions are to be attributed not to their own natural disposition, but to the very shameful manner in which they have on most unprovoked grounds been treated. I trust you will, with me, consider Mr. Batman's plan, one from which much good is likely to result, and submit it for the consideration of His Excellency the Lieut. Governor, who I am sure will not withhold his sanction and assistance in any case where a benefit might result to those unhappy creatures".*

*[Margin note: Letter dated 15 June 1829 addressed to Major Gray. J.P.]*[cxl]

William Gray also pursued other avenues and was not short of ideas, no matter how bizarre. In June 1829 he supported the idea of introducing New Zealand Maoris to VDL to assist their cause as Maoris 'were then regarded as about the most blood-thirsty savages and cannibals that the world could furnish' and would willingly and easily catch 'Black-Fellows'. Not surprisingly Governor Arthur rejected the idea with well- grounded fears of a massacre.[cxli] Reprisals began in earnest on both sides. In 1830 a one of James Gray's Shepherds was speared and on the 24th of September William Tidy was killed on Major Gray's property. In February 1829 it was reported that 'Nine were killed and three taken, near St. Paul's River, ten days back, and about the same time ten were shot and two taken, near the Eastern Marshes.' [cxlii]

In 1830 a survey was conducted in relation to the conflicts with the Aborigines. It included the question;

"To what causes would you attribute the rise and progress of the hostility displayed by the Natives? "

Although there were a variety of responses to this Gray (Avoca)[cxliii] and others believed that the Aborigines had been provoked by various brutal actions.[cxliv]

This shows a little of Gray's personal conflict during this time. On the one hand he could understand that the Aborigines had been provoked into their actions while on the other he was clearly concerned for the safety of his family and neighbours. At times he tried to engage with the tribes, and met with a group sheltering at Batman's property,

According to Major Gray, who visited Batman's farm they seemed willing to stay. Conversations with their Chief, Limogana, led Gray to hope that the tribe could be induced to co-operate and bring in further Aborigines. Gray spoke enthusiastically of the tribesmen, describing them as "cheerful and of good stature.[cxlv]

Such enthusiasm was short lived as the tribe moved on, taking Batman's knives and dogs while leaving the gifts of blankets and clothes which displays so aptly the total misa-lignment of cultural values and the trials afforded any attempt at some form of peaceful coexistence. In October three of Major Gray's servants were killed and another seriously wounded. The Colonial Times reported; the men in question were at work at a little distance from their hut, when the Natives rushed on them, and beat them to death with their wad-dies. They afterwards disfigured them in a most shocking manner, cutting the heads off of three of them, and placing them between their legs.[cxlvi]

Perhaps the last details should be read with a degree of caution. Truth and War are generally incompatible, especially when seen in the context of the times.

The atrocities on both sides continued It really was a war for survival as noted by Desailly.

There was worse to come. On November 1, Gray reported that many robberies had taken place in the area of Batman's farm. Two attacking Aborigines had been shot . Gray was now attempting to determine if one of them belonged to the run-away tribe....

On November 11, Gray reported that his worst suspicions had been confirmed. The body of an Aborigine had been found and identified as "one of those ungrateful savages who came to Batman's.[cxlvii]

The whole community were now in a state of fear and desperation which led Major Gray to express the views of many when he wrote to Governor Arthur on the 29th August;

*the present state of continual terror which appears to have Seized upon the minds of almost every individual . . . particularly those in the remote districts, who are looking forward with fearful anxiety to the approaching fine weather which will no doubt be attended with bloodshed, if their [Aboriginal] progress be not speedily arrested.*[cxlviii]

Gray went on to develop and promote the idea of the 'Black Line' which Arthur was only too willing to accept. McMahon (1995 p44) documented Major Gray's involvement;

Gray proposed a maximum co-ordinated effort involving civilian search parties aided by the military, simultaneously operating in all police districts, which would convince the Aborigines "that their only safety consisted in their accepting . . . offers of reconciliation . . . or in eventually capturing" them.[cxlix]

Arthur eventually accepted Gray's idea of the Black Line and the *levy en masse* (Conscription of civilians)[cl] proclaimed on the 9th September 1830. In later reminiscences of the Black War by an unknown leader recounted another attack on Major Gray. I have visited the place and travelled along the same marsh at Major Gray's at Avoca four men were engaged putting up a log fence, the blacks came down on the man felling the tree, speared him, and then attached the one driving the bullocks, who experienced the same fate, and then they speared the remaining two, who were at work putting up the fence, the blacks were not satisfied by spearing, but always used their waddies in breaking every bone.[cli]

Humphrey Grey and his family had arrived a few months earlier and he must have wondered what he had bought his family to when, in September, they were surrounded by Aborigines at their home, Eastbourne.

It was probably part of the same tribe to which these belonged who subsequently surrounded and attacked the premises of Mr. Humphrey Grey in the same neighbourhood, and kept the whole family in a state of danger and alarm for 4 or 5 hours, until they were ultimately driven off. [clii]

The barn on Eastbourne was clearly designed for protection against attack, with small slits and a secure door which may have saved the family on that day if it had been completed.

*Figure 82 Barn at Eastbourne*

The Grey family were attacked a further two times in October. Shortly after, in October 'a party of four Blacks was overtaken last week near Major Gray's at St. Paul's plains, but being so thoroughly smeared with opossum grease, three of them contrived to make their escape.'[cliii] Clearly there are many more records related to this topic which are readily available. The purpose of this section is to provide a small insight into the conflict and the associated values and attitudes of the times with specific reference to the experiences of just one family. It is obviously given from their point of view, a family whose culture and understanding of the World was **unequivocally em-**bedded in 19th Century British culture.

# Battles between the Tyerrernotepanner (Stoney Creek people) and the Gray families at Avoca, VDL 1829 -1832

(E) Humphrey Grey and family attacked by Aborigines and kept the whole family in a state of danger for 4-5 hours before being driven off. The Hobart Town Courier, Saturday 25 September 1830, p.2S

Battles between the Tyerrernotepanner (Stoney Creek people) and the Gray families at Avoca, VDL 1829 -1832 (R) 2n April 1829 Moses Garcia (SHP) killed by(R) 9th

(R) 28th. Sept Three men, at Major Grey's, wounded by natives, and one dangerously wounded with stones.

(G) 28th May 1831 attacked by Aborigines

(R) 29th Aug William writes to Gov Arthur the present state of continual terror which appears to have Seized upon the minds of almost every individual . . . . particularly those in the remote districts, who are looking forward with fearful anxiety to the approaching fine weather which will no doubt be attended with bloodshed, if their [Aboriginal] progress be not *speedily arrested*

(R) April 1829, a party of Aboriginal people attacked a hut on Major William Gray's property at St Paul's Plains. Two of Gray's shepherds were injured in the attack, one receiving nine spears in his back besides other wounds.7 Ryan and Avoca bridge plan. Bonwick, J. (1884). *The lost Tasmanian race*

(R) 2n April 1829 Moses Garcia (SHP) killed by Aborigines

24th September William Tidy killed by Aborigines on Gray property

(E) 17th Oct 2 SW attacked for 2 hours

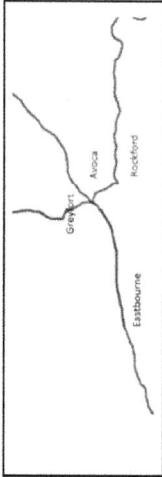

Aborigines at St Pauls River where nine of his people were killed. Nine were killed and three taken, near St. Paul's River, ten days back. (1829,

Aborigines at St Pauls Plains. Two of Gray's shepherds were injured in the attack, one receiving nine spears in his back besides other wounds. 7 Ryan and Avoca bridge plan.

(R) 9th Sept 1830 William suggests 'Black Line to Arthur.

(R) 9th Feb 1829 A massacre occurred close by at St Pauls River where nine of his people were killed. Nine were killed and three taken, near St. Paul's River, ten days back [No heading]. (1829, February 9). *Launceston*

CODE: (R) Rockford; (E) Eastbourne; (G) Grayfort

(R) Oct A party of four Blacks was overtaken last week near Major Gray's at St. Paul's plains, but being so thoroughly smeared with opossum grease, three of them contrived to make their escape. *The Hobart Town Courier*, Saturday 16 October 1830.

June William supports idea of bringing in Maoris' to quell the Aborigines.

(G) 1830 2nd Sheppard wounded by Aborigines - speared

Feb 1829 A massacre occurred close by (R) April 1829, a party of Aboriginal people attacked a hut on Major William Gray's property at St Paul's

(E) 30th Oct 1830 Sheppard attacked

(G) 1830 2nd Sheppard wounded by Aborigines

Captain Gray, of Avoca, was often seen standing over his threshold with a loaded musket.

(R) 7th Oct BLACK LINE.

Roving Parties under Mr. Batman, and will receive the most effectual cooperation from Major Gray, who will, no doubt, be warmly, seconded by Messrs. Legge, Talbot, Grant, Smith, Gray, Hepburn, Kearney, Bates, and all other Settlers.

**The next generation: Sarah Elizabeth Grey and Fredrick Maitland Innes.**

It goes without saying that families are made up of individuals and as Jane Austen's *Emma* so astutely points out;

It is very unfair to judge of any body's conduct, without an intimate knowledge of their situation. Nobody, who has not been in the interior of a family, can say what the difficulties of any individual of that family maybe.[cliv]

The previous section intimated that the Gray family as a whole all thought alike and in no way challenged the values and conventions which were so much part of their everyday life. In this case the terrible conflict and war with the Aborigines. Sarah Elizabeth Grey, (Lysbeth) Humphrey and Catherine's youngest daughter, leaves us with some insight into the social conflicts of the day and her own questioning and enquiring mind.

In 1838, at the age of 17, Sarah married Frederick Maitland Innes at Eastbourne. He had only been in the colony for a short time but soon after the marriage had to return to Scotland to care for his sick mother. Sarah travelled alone to England in 1841 to be with him. The trade winds took the ships from VDL around Cape Horn and then north-east to their first port of call at St Helena. The letter written by Sarah from the Island is presented in full in the Appendix A. It shows considerable intellect, thoughtfulness and a maturity of social inquiry especially for a young woman of twenty in that era. In it she discusses her reaction to the slave trade which was a thriving trade in the 1840s.

On her arrival in London Lysbeth is described by John Quain in a letter to his mother;

Of middle size, light hair, approaching almost to sandy, smart, pretty figure, intelligent countenance, very pleasing, affectionate, in short, Irish manner coupled with an agreeable, lively, but shrewd method of expressing herself, which is taking in the extreme.[clv]

Growing up in Avoca during the 1830s and being faced with the realities of the war with the Aboriginal people Lysbeth Grey had clearly developed her own, independent, social conscience and was willing to express her ideas. She would no doubt have been a match for Cousin William's uncompromising intellect. It is easy to see why she was so attracted, intellectually and emotionally to Frederick. As a new arrival in VDL in the late 1830s he must have been confronted by what he saw and heard about the treatment of the Aborigines. When in London he became the secretary of the Aborigines' Protection Society (APS) which aimed 'to assist in protecting the defenceless and promoting the advancement of 'Uncivilized Tribes' by guiding colonial policy through the publication of materials and the mobilization of 'popular opinion'.[clvi]

It was closely allied with movements against slavery and the Innes were part of that circle of thought and social change. As with any challenge to conventional thinking this was indeed a difficult and at times impossible journey. The juggernaut of the massive convict transportation, white settlers arriving and the might of the British Empire was seemingly unstoppable. However it must be said that Lysbeth, Frederick and many others at least tried to affect change in the way of thinking toward the Aboriginal community, a debate which is still very much alive today.

**President.**
Sir THOMAS FOWELL BUXTON, Bart.

**Committee.**

| | |
|---|---|
| WILLIAM ALLEN, Esq. | W. M. HIGGINS, Esq. |
| G. F. ANGAS, Esq. | T. HODGKIN, Esq. M.D. |
| WILLIAM ALDAM, Jun. Esq. | M. HUTCHINSON, Jun. Esq. |
| E. BAINES, Esq. M.P. | A. JOHNSTON, Esq. |
| J. BEAUMONT, Esq. | R. KING, Esq. |
| ROBERT BELL, Esq. | Rt. Hon. Sir S. LUSHINGTON, M.P. |
| JOHN IVATT BRISCOE, Esq. M.P. | C. LUSHINGTON, Esq. M.P. |
| Sir JEREMIAH BRYANT. | F. LUCAS, Esq. |
| Rev. JOHN BURNETT. | R. M. MARTIN, Esq. |
| E. N. BUXTON, Esq. | HENRY MOREING, Esq. |
| R. CHAPMAN, Esq. | STANDISH MOTTE, Esq. |
| W. CLAY, Esq. | DANIEL O'CONNELL, Esq. M.P. |
| Rev. F. CUNNINGHAM, M.A. | J. PEASE, Esq. |
| Sir AUGUSTUS D'ESTE, Bart. | J. PEASE, Esq. M.P. |
| W. EVANS, Esq. M.P. | HENRY ROBARTS, Esq. |
| W. E. FORSTER, Esq. | CHARLES STURGEON, Esq. |
| Rev. J. J. FREEMAN. | HULL TERRELL, Esq. |
| S. GURNEY, Jun. Esq. | J. H. TREGOOLD, Esq. |
| A. HEAVISIDE, Esq. | H. TUCKETT, Esq. |
| C. HINDLEY, Esq. M.P. | Captain JOHN WASHINGTON, R.N. |
| GURNEY HOARE, Esq. | Rev. A. WELLS. |
| ROBERT HOWARD, Esq. | S. WILKIN, Esq. |

**Treasurer.**
HENRY TUCKETT, Esq.
No. 7, South Street, Finsbury.

**Secretary.**
F. MAITLAND INNES, Esq.
Beaufort Buildings, Strand.

## ABORIGINES' PROTECTION SOCIETY.

OFFICE, No. 17, BEAUFORT BUILDINGS, STRAND.

*Opposite to Exeter Hall.*

The object of this Society is to assist in protecting the defenceless, and promoting the advancement of uncivilized Tribes.

A Subscription of One Guinea a Year, or a Donation of Ten Pounds, constitutes a Member.

The Society is desirous of promoting the formation of Auxiliary Associations, both at home and abroad.

Subscriptions or Donations in aid of the Funds of the Society will be thankfully received by the Treasurer, the Secretaries, or any Member of the Committee.

### HONORARY MEMBERS.

#### BRITISH.

| | |
|---|---|
| Abbot, George, Esq. | Mitchell, Rev. D. Glasgow. |
| Banim, John, Esq. Kilkenny. | Medhurst, Rev. W. H. China. |
| Brown, John, Esq. South Australia. | Moffatt, Rev. R. Lattakoo. |
| Campbell, T. Esq. | Morgan, Captain. |
| Deverell, W. R. Esq. | Morrison, John, Esq. |
| Elliott, Ebenezer, Esq. | Pears, Rev. J. Cape Town. |
| Elliott, Rev. J. Cape of Good Hope. | Philip, Rev. Dr. Cape Town. |
| Fairburn, John, Esq. Cape Town. | Philip, Mrs. Cape of Good Hope. |
| Grey, Lieut. G. | Prichard, Dr. Bristol. |
| Hack, Barton, Adelaide Settlement, South Australia. | Prichard, G. Esq. Tahiti. |
| | Read, Rev. James, Kat River. |
| Halliday, Miss, Egypt. | Read, Rev. J. jun. ditto. |
| Herschell, Sir John, Bart. F.R.S. &c. | Ritchie, Leitch, Esq. |
| Hill, R. Esq. Jamaica. | Robson, Mrs. Cape of Good Hope. |
| Howitt, William, Esq. | Ryerson, Rev. Egerton, Upper Canada. |
| Johnson, Mr. Bombay. | Saunders, Rev. John, Cape of Good Hope. |
| Jones, Rev. Peter, Canada. | |
| Kennedy, William, Esq. Hull. | Shaw, Rev. W. Caffreland. |
| Kerr, Colonel, Canada. | Smith, Dr. Andrew, Cape Town. |
| Machonochie, Capt. R.N. | Snow, Rev. Mr. South Australia. |
| Mair, Patrick, Esq. | Tomas, Lieut. R.N. |
| Marsden, Rev. S. New South Wales. | Wilks, Rev. M. Paris. |
| Marsden, Miss, ditto. | Wright, Rev. P. Griqua Town. |
| Miles, Rev. Mr. Montreal. | Wright, Rev. Dr. Paris. |

# BOX ELEVEN: A NEW WAY OF LIFE BEGINS

The brutal war with the Aborigines was now over for the Europeans living in Avoca. The British had won. Their victory was absolute, decisive and final: leaving a hollow silence in the surrounding hills and valleys. The new inhabitants were now safe on their freshly claimed land to live and transplant an alien cultural identity on the Island. The family were very much imbued with the norms, ethics and manners associated with Protestant England. While they had all been born in Ireland and for several generations before, the Gray family most certainly regarded Ireland as part of Britain, both legally and morally. Ireland had become part of Great Britain ruled by Westminster since the Act of Union in 1801

With this in mind it is easy to see how each family made decisions and adapted to their new environment. In a way, it was seen as a struggle, a battle against foreign surroundings which needed to be tamed and controlled to suit their farming needs. The government rewarded farmers who 'developed' their land, including fencing, which seemed such a strange concept of imposing straight lines and artificial boundaries on an untouched landscape. Clearing the land of trees and wild animals was also a priority to make way for European farming practices and stock, including sheep, cattle, pigs, chickens, dogs, horses, bullocks, rabbits and similarly invasive flora and fauna were introduced. Native animals were seen as pests and many species were eliminated before the century was over.

When the Grays arrived the Thylacine, Emu and many other native animals existed in the vicinity of their homesteads, as shown in the quote by Colonel Legge (1845) cited by *H Stuart Dove* in The Tasmanian Emu 1924.[clvii]

-- --

" As regards the former, it may be interesting to members of the A.O.U. to hear that during the 'forties the Tasmanian Emu used to inhabit, and bred regularly in, a locality known as Kearney's Bogs. This upland moor was part of the Rockfort estate, owned then by the writer's father-in-law, Major W. Gray. It is situated about 12 miles to the south of Avoca, in a portion of the Eastcoast Ranges, which flank the valley of the St. Paul's River. One of the shepherds of the estate, H. Wyburn, was resident at the bogs, and used not infrequently to bring eggs to the house, and about the year 1845 succeeded in capturing two young birds, which were conveyed to Rockfort and reared in the goose-yard. They lived about the homestead for several years, and were tame and mischievous, coming to the open French windows of the dining-room to be fed, thrusting their heads into the room at times. Mrs. Legge, who was then a young girl, has vivid recollections of these Emus, and avers that they were large birds, very similar to those of the continent. Some years afterwards a pair of Tasmanian Emus, which I am

Overall the economy was strong and an ideal time to be farming and exporting products such as wool, meat, grains and so on. With convict labour,

abundant land and a modicum of business sense it would be hard not to make a financial success.

The 1830s in VDL were a boom time for the early settlers. The European population was growing rapidly, wheat and other supplies were in high demand both locally as well as for NSW. The English woollen mills delighted in the quality of wool from the Colony and farmers were able to sell anything they produced. With free land grants prior to 1830 many were well established by this time and with a constant supply of convict labour both free settlers and pardoned or ticket of leave convicts were in a prime position to mark out a comfortable living from the land Humphrey Grey as we know was a natural and successful businessman and he seemed readily able to translate his skills into farming.[clviii]

Eastbourne was prime land with a constant water supply. It was flat and sparsely wooded which made for easy pasture and his sheep flocks flourished.

---

**SHEEP.**

THE undersigned has four hundred Fine Woolled EWES FOR SALE.

HUMPHREY GRAY.

St. Paul's Plains,
April 11, 1836.

---

He may have produced wheat but many were at the time and he may well have diversified into crops. His achievements in farming are most evident with the sale of 400 sheep in both 1836 and 37 as shown in the Launceston Advertiser.

He obviously felt secure enough in 1840 to support the Emigration Scheme and assist people to migrate and work for him. This was largely due to the fact that the convict assignment system had stopped in 1840 and the colonists now realised they had a labour shortage. The scheme aimed to bring skilled workers to the Colony in areas where there were shortages. Many were desperate to start a new life and

during the boom years over 5000 assisted migrants set out from England to make a new life in VDL.

---

**THE GAZETTE.**

FRIDAY MORNING, August 7, 1840.

GOVERNMENT NOTICE, No. 196, Colonial Secretary's Office, August 5.

The Lieutenant-Governor directs it to be notified to the under-mentioned individuals, that their applications for Emigrants, under the terms of the Government Notice of the 14th May last, have been received, and will be transmitted by the first opportunity to T. F. Elliot, Esquire, Agent-General for Emigration, No. 2, Middle Scotland Yard, London, with a request that he will afford every information to all applicants, and instruct his agents at the several outports at which such Emigrants are proposed to be selected or embarked to do the same.

Edwin Boultbee, James Corbett, Walter Davidson, Thomas Diprose, William Gray, Humphrey Grey, George Frederick Goble, David Gibson, John Gibson, John Leake, Simeon Lord, James M'Jarrett, John M'Leod, Matthew Muir, Adam Robertson, Adolphus Frederic Rooke, Francis W. Von Steiglitz, Frederic Coape Smith, Archibald Smith, William Gardner Sams, Theophilus Smith, James Thomson, Jocelyn Thomas, Richard H. Willis, John West, James B. Whitehead.

By His Excellency's command,
M. FORSTER.

THE GAZETTE

FRIDAY MORNING, August 7<sup>th</sup> 1840

*.... The Lieutenant-Governor directs it to be notified to The undermentioned individuals that their applications for Emigrants have been received .... [and approved] ....William Gray, Humphrey Grey.....*

*By His Excellency's command, M Forester..* [clix]

> County of Glamorgan.—Parish of Eastbourne, comprising the township of Eastbourne Reserve, lot 183, 640 acres, at £1 per acre, £640, upset price, Humphrey Gray.
> The attendance was thin, and the amount of the sale only £741.

Undeterred by the economic recession Humphrey continued to build up his assets and purchased more crown land in 1845, an astute move when demand was low and prices low. Only nine lots sold of the fifty-six on offer and few people were at the sale. [clx]

Each family settled down to working their land and pursuing personal and pleasurable quests.

The family were constantly under threat from bushrangers and thieves who lived a life on the run and viewed wealthy landowners as a reasonable source of material gain. Frequently though they were armed and dangerous. In June 1834 Eastbourne was the target of three armed men attacked the shepherd's in their hut.[clxi]

Improbable as it may seem two bullocks were stolen from Eastbourne in July 1835. It is hard to imagine how such a slow lumbering beast could be whisked away and hidden especially with such distinctive branding for all to see.

> all my sheep. Mr. Humphrey Grey's place was robbed last Friday night by 3 armed men, they tied the men in the hut and then helped themselves to what they wanted in the house. (This is within three miles of a magistrate, furnished with his proper complement of constables, we shall be glad to learn what success has been met with in capturing the rogues).

Even so bullocks could travel up to 25 kilometres a day depending on the terrain. They were valuable and essential for all manner of activities including transporting large quantities of goods and people, for ploughing, pulling out trees and in fact most things a modern day tractor would do. They remained the main form of transport in VDL until the railways were introduced in the mid-19th Century. For Humphrey, it would have been an costly and inconvenient loss and effectively stopped much of the heavy work on the farm and hence his offer of a reward. Ten pounds would have been quite a sum at this time.[clxii]

> ### TEN POUNDS REWARD.
>
> STOLEN from the undersigned, 2 Bullocks, 1 red, T-C on each hip and HG on the horn, the other black and white, branded R-I near hip and HG near shoulder. Any person giving such information as may lead to the conviction of the offender or offenders will receive the above reward.
>
> HUMPHREY GRAY.
>
> St. Paul's plains, July 4.

and went off from the place. About eight months ago, I was at Major Gray's shepherd's hut, and took away two guns. There were two men in the hut : I

About eight months ago, I was at Major Gray's shepherd's hut, and took away two guns.

There were two men in the hut I was joined by another man- we got up to the hut before they saw us, and told them we would blow their brains out if they moved. The same night we went to Mr. Humphrey Gray's hut-we saw two men there we went there to m -resistance was made one of the men seized hold of my gun, and my mate fired at him, and hit him under the arm, and afterwards levelled his empty piece at the other man, and frightened him; they had no guns ; I did not see what became of the wounded man, for we left the hut immediately ; I heard at several places he was dead, but did not know it for certain until I heard it at Nash's house.

*ake a damper*

Occasionally though the threat became deadly. In the following year, Henry Hunt escaped from the Wedge survey team and spent some months roaming and stealing from the setters in the area. In his confession, he tells howhe stole two guns from Major Gray's shepherd's hut and then proceeded to Eastbourne where an altercation took place h Humphrey Grey's convict shepherd, possibly James Brigg, who was murdered. Hunt was also responsible for killing Captain Sergeantson. Meetings were held in Campbell Town, rewards for capture raised including subscriptions from all the Grays. These are Hunt's words reported from his trial. clxiii

ago, I was at Major Gray's shepherd's hut, and took away two guns. There were two men in the hut; I I was joined by another man—we got up to the hut before they saw us, and told them we would blow their brains out if they moved. The same night we went to Mr. Humphrey Gray's hut—we saw two men there—we went there to make a damper—resistance was made—one of the men seized hold of my gun, and my mate fired at him, and hit him under the arm, and afterwards levelled his empty piece at the other man, and frightened him ; they had no guns ; I did not see what became of the wounded man, for we left the hut immediately ; I heard at several places he was dead, but did not know it for certain until I heard it at Nash's house. I was going

## Yeomanry: The Campbell Town Mounted Volunteers

To overcome the problem of bushrangers it will come as no surprise that Major William's response was military in nature. Grand, rather ill-conceived and not entirely successful schemes had been a hall mark of his career: these included the ill-fated African expeditions and the Black Line in VDL.

Undeterred, he and a few of his like-minded aging soldiers including George Keach ('Chiswick') and Arthur Leake ('Ashby') met in Campbelltown to form their own

Yeomanry. For those unfamiliar with the term, Yeomanry are groups of men who held and cultivated small estates in England and were called upon as a volunteer cavalry force when needed.

They were to be called Campbell Town Mounted Volunteers and were imbued

However, I am proud to see so many of the junior branches of the district around me. Your readiness on the present occasion is most creditable. I can assure you, when old age creeps on, you will look back *upon the present time as one of the proudest periods of your lives, for what can be more praiseworthy than endeavouring to restore safely to the firesides of your brother settlers, and more especially, shielding that sex, without whose safety, man's life would be a mere blank?*

*I need not tell you, young men, that in days of old, the smiles of lovely woman led to deeds of great daring, and rest assured your present spirited and manly intentions will gain you the good-will of all the young ladies of the district, and the approbation of their mothers.*

with all the vigour and fighting spirit of young men one could rouse by Mr Henry Keach on a Saturday afternoon at M'Kay's Inn on the 13th April 1844.[clxiv] The full text is well worth reading in its entirety but the section here will provide a little of its depth of feeling and the tenor of Keach's speech. The Yeomanry was to be run on military lines and each member was to 'hold himself in readiness to commence duty with horse, arms, and ammunition, and carry such provisions as he may think proper, at any hour of the day or night, without distinction'.

Those closest to Avoca were to assemble at Major Gray's Rockford immediately after hearing of bushrangers in the district. Needless to say the Governor of the day, Eardley Wilmot was not overly keen to have an armed militia roaming around the country enforcing the law to their own satisfaction and immediately put an end to the noble intentions of the Campbell Town Mounted Volunteers. Although it should be noted that attacks by bushrangers, now called robbery-under-arms, continued for many years to come. These included an armed robbery and murder at Simeon Lord's, Bona Vista in 1853 and an attack on Eastbourne in 1858.[clxv]

MURDER AND ROBBERIES UNDER ARMS NEAR AVOCA. —From an extract from a private letter received in town this morning we learn that a report has been received at Campbell Town of another dreadful murder somewhere near Avoca. The unfortunate victim is the late Mr. Duxbury's brother. He had remained in charge of a hut while the owner was away in the bush; upon the latter returning he found Mr. Duxbury gone, and the hut rifled of its covetable contents. Eventually the body was found quite stripped, his watch, money, and clothes having been taken away. We glean from the same source that robberies under arms have been committed at Mr. Humphrey Gray's and at Mr. Youl's.

Murder and Robberies Under Arms near Avoca

-From an extract from a private letter received in town this morning we learn that a report has been received at Campbell Town of another dreadful murder somewhere near Avoca.

This unfortunate victim is the late Mr. Duxbury's brother. He had remained in charge of a hut while the owner was away in the bush: upon the latter returning he found Mr. Duxbury gone, and the hut rifled of its covetable contents. Eventually the body was found quite stripped, his watch, money, and clothes having been taken away. We glean from the same source that robberies under arms been committed at Mr. Humphrey Grey's and at Mr Youl's.

# BOX THIRTEEN: CONVICTS AND THE GRAY FAMILIES

The English convict system needs to be considered in the context of the times. Great Britain was in the midst of massive social, political and economic upheaval from the late 1700s. The Industrial Revolution had transformed the nation from a rural based society to one which created wealth through both agrarian and industrial innovation and brilliant engineering.

Canals crisscrossed the countryside for the first time, allowing raw materials to be transported easily and cheaply to port cities where factories mass produced goods both for export and to satisfy local needs. While the nation and individuals profited, many more became dependent on money as their sole means of survival. No money meant no food, no shelter. Thousands moved to the cities, either through displacement from the Agrarian Revolution or the desire to make a living in the urban quagmire of 19th century cities such as London, Manchester and Liverpool. There was also a significant increase in population.

In addition the French Revolution was not far from the minds of the ruling classes in England, who were quick to quash any thought of allowing the 'great unwashed' to gain any semblance of political influence by the acquisition of adult suffrage.[clxvi]

The result of such upheaval was evidenced in the huge numbers of people living in dire poverty. Under different circumstances the vast majority would have lived their lives within the law but hunger is a great motivator for crime.

It should be taken into account too that most of the convicts sent to VDL committed petty crimes, those who stole over five pounds worth of goods were executed. Exemplified by Sarah Esp, who was transported for seven years for stealing an apron and assigned to Major Gray and Humphrey,. Most convicts simply wanted to do their time and get on with making a family and living as best they could. Interestingly, over 70,000 people were sent to VDL in the first 50 years of settlement. However after the 1850s thousands of people left the colony in search of gold in Victoria. This resulted in a quiet and safe community in the newly named Tasmania which became a most law abiding Colony in the British Empire for several decades.

Those who stayed in Tasmania, mainly had families, and worked and lived their lives in peace with much better prospects than if they had stayed in England. Free settlers certainly regarded it as their right to have convicts assigned to them as they carved out farms, built fine houses and created a very English lifestyle in this foreign land.

The Gray families had several convicts assigned to them during this time. These were people too who had their own traumas, dreams and human desires. It is all too easy to classify convicts as being all the same; they were not and neither were their destinies. During the research for this book, the author had contact with several descendants of those mentioned below. More information about each one can be easily researched in the Tasmanian Archives and other sources.

The following people were assigned to different members of the Gray family at Avoca;

## Convicts assigned to Humphrey Gray

### Briggs Brothers

The three Briggs brothers, Christopher,[clxvii] James [clxviii] and Charles[clxix]were transported on the 600 ton Gilmore, which left London on 27th November 1831 and arrived in Hobart on 22nd March 1832 with 222 male prisoners. Christopher was assigned to W Brodribb and James and Charles to Humphrey Grey.

The assignment appears to have been successful with the brothers remaining at Eastbourne for some years until the 26th October 1835 when James was 'shot by some person unknown'. (Convict record). This may well have been the bushranger Henry Hunt who also killed Captain Sergeantson. James' brother Christopher married and their descendants continue the family name today, one of whom is Frank James Briggs.

### Sarah Esp[clxx] (proper name Julia Esp; uxor Sarah Kerr)

Sarah arrived in 1839 aged 29. She was illiterate, had a pale complexion, 5ft 2 and three quarters in height, brown eye lashes, hazel eyes and had a quiet nature. Being Irish and Catholic will have made her journey challenging in the staunch cultural and Protestant environment of the Gray households. She was assigned to Major Gray for a few months and then to Humphrey who, according to the 1841 muster, appears to have been residing in Launceston.

During this time she became pregnant and was returned to the Crown on the 2nd August 1842. She gave birth to Amelia at the infamous Launceston female factory in October. Sarah was given a ticket of leave in 1843 and once married, lived for many years in Campbell Town before going to Victoria in 1847.

A fuller account of Sarah's life is available in *Patchwork Prisoners* by *Trudy Cowley & Dianne Snowden*[clxxi]

### Elizabeth Gerrand[clxxii]

At 18 Elizabeth, from Aberdeen, was four foot, eleven and three quarters of an inch high, oval face, dark eyed, red head and freckles. Sentenced at Perth on the 26th April 1852 for theft and arrived in VDL a year later. Her career was to say the least

> ROBBERY BY A SERVANT. —Elizabeth Gerrand was charged by Detective Bryon, of the Rural Police, with stealing, on the 7th instant, at Avoca, one £5 note, one silk dress, value £4, and other articles, the property of her master, Humphrey Grey. The prisoner was remanded to Avoca.

colourful, perhaps suggesting a youthful and feisty personality, beginning with being charged with being under the influence of liquor and leaving her bedroom window open for unlawful purposes – 14 days in the cells. Soon after, she was charged with using obscene language and given 9 months hard labour. Her life continued for years in a similar vein until she stole 'one five pound note, a silk dress, value £4 and other articles' from the Grey family in January 1859.[clxxiii]

### Convicts assigned to Major Gray

### Eliza Orrell[cxxix]

Eliza was a woman in her thirties with bright auburn hair, light blue eyes and a feisty disposition who was clearly determined to fight the system every inch of the way. On one occasion, she was charged by Major Gray with using abusive and obscene language and with being absent all night.[cxxx] Standing up to William showed either great daring or perhaps a degree of recklessness. She was returned to second class at the House of Correction and was reassigned.

However in April 1836, still as a convict, she married Henry Smith in Launceston and appears to have largely stayed out of trouble after her marriage. [cxxxi]

### Jane Raydon[clxxiv]

Jane, tall, with a dark complexion, dark brown hair and brown eyes worked as a housemaid and needle woman. Married in England she was sentenced to life for stealing. Jane was only with Major Gray for a short time, when she was returned to the Crown "under peculiar circumstances" [cxxxii] In 1841, Jane, a widow by then, married Edmund Baker, although shortly afterward she was once again in trouble after committing a felony and was resentenced.

## Alice Sullivan[clxxv]

Alice's story has been researched and written by her GGG granddaughter Veronica Hayes whose family still reside in Ballarat.

Born in Sligo, a small village on the West Coast of Ireland in 1817, blue- eyed with dark brown hair, Alice Sullivan somehow found herself in 1840 at Lancaster Liverpool Quarter Sessions. At the age of twenty three, she was convicted of "Robbery Simple". Alice received a ten year conviction and transportation to Van Diemen's Land for stealing a watch. She arrived in Hobart on the 17th January 1841 aboard the *Navarino*. She is described as being 5ft 1", having a fresh complexion in an oval face, with a rather large mouth and the distinguishing feature of a burnt right hand and a crooked little finger. Growing up in Sligo she probably spoke Gaelic as her first language and appears to have had little education, as she was unable to write her name.

Alice was assigned to Major Gray in Avoca as a servant upon arrival and is recorded at Rockford in the 1841 muster. On 30 May 1842, Alice was recorded as a nurse and wed James Whyburn, butcher. The union is recorded as the first official marriage in the then brand new St Thomas' Church, a fact Alice's great, great, great granddaughter, Veronica Hayes, was delighted to discover when visiting Avoca and Rockford some 173 years later.After five years and seven months in the colony, Alice was pardoned "having completed above 6 years of a 10 year sentence and no complaint whatsoever having been made against her from the time of her arrival."

Alice and James welcomed a son, James junior, in 1845. Two years later, the family was living in Frederick St Launceston when young James sadly passed away. The trail of Alice becomes a little hard to follow here. There is evidence to suggest she may have returned to Ireland and re-married in Belfast.

Alice is then found back in Australia on the Ballarat goldfields in 1858, giving birth, alone, to her own daughter Alice and known as Mrs John Knight, midwife.

## James Lambert[clxxvi]

James would have been an asset to Major Gray. His skills as a farmer, ploughman and timber feller were valuable in the early years of establishing the settlements. Being Protestant certainly appealed to Gray as well as his obvious desire to bring his family out to VDL. James came from Dorsetshire, England and had worked for the Butts of Motcombe. Transported for stealing barley he arrived at about the same time as the Gray brothers, although in different circumstances. James settled in well and soon managed to bring his family out to be with him in the early 1830s, including his adult daughter who had a child, Maria Lambert, in 1832. Maria was christened in the Gray house with William's daughter Elizabeth, indicating a close relationship between the families.

Mrs Maria Raake, as she became,[clxxvii] lived to her centenary year and in 1932 shared her story with the *Mercury* Newspaper. She describes her delightful, although at times dangerous, story of growing up at Avoca and her early days at Rockford.[clxxviii] She was a greatly loved bush nurse and midwife for decades in the Fingal Valley. James became the manager or proprietor on Simeon Lord's estate

*Bona Vista* hence his encounter with Dalton and Hunt, notorious bushrangers who murdered Constable Buckmaster. Maria's home remains on the Benham Estate and is still referred to as the Raake House.

### William Little[clxxix]

William arrived with James on the *Asia* in December 1827 and was assigned to Major Gray. Within a few years he was living at Westbury and died as a result of an accident on 1st March 1831 aged 37.

### Sarah Taylor [clxxx]

At 23, Sarah was petite at just over 5ft, with fair complexion, brown hair and grey eyes. She was considered to have an industrious disposition and probably worked in Major Gray's house as a lady's maid and dressmaker. Sarah is recorded in the 1841 muster as living in Avoca in the service of Major Gray.[cxxxviii]

In all likelihood, there were more convicts working for the Gray families at various times especially during peak times such as house construction and other ventures.

However it is clear that Major Gray had by far the greater numbers of convicts assigned to him while far fewer were assigned to James and Humphrey. The explanation for this is perhaps lies in the character and disposition of each of the three.

The Major was industrious, ambitious and willing to exploit every opportunity available to him, including the use of convict labour. He also had a fearsome reputation for punishment and harsh treatment of those in his charge, which may explain the rapid and continuous change of convicts at *Rockford*. Humphrey and James were also assigned convicts from time to time. For example in 1838, convicts were sent from Willis' Corner to all three Gray families.[clxxxi]

Humphrey also had the Barnes' and other servants who were free and chose to work for the family. Perhaps his more measured approach encouraged a stronger sense of loyalty and diligence.

### End of Transportation

The history of the Anti-Transportation movement is well documented and need not be repeated here other than to note that the Gray families had a keen interest in the outcome. While transportation to VDL ended in 1853, it was not without a fight on the part of many in the Colony including Major Gray. The debate stretched over decades parliamentary committees enquiring into the convict system.

The reaction to the Select Committee of the House of Commons in 1839, which recommended its termination, was a vocal public meeting in Launceston with Major Gray appointed to the committee. The result was a petition to Her Majesty the Queen on the 27 March, which included the signature of Major Gray representing Avoca and the South Esk. But Petitioners rest their prayer, not only on the injury to them and their families which any great and sudden change would entail, but on the danger which they think they can see resulting therefrom to important national interests. Under all these circumstances, it is the humble prayer of Petitioners that Her Majesty will not sanction the adoption of any measure having for its object to abolish the System of Transportation, coupled with Assignment, as the national system of Secondary Punishment.[clxxxii]

There were many benefits of transportation for the upper classes such as the acquisition of extensive personal property and unprecedented prosperity as well as religious and moral benefits;

The want of adequate religious instruction was perceived as the greatest failure of the  Transportation

System in past years; yet perhaps no system offers a better opportunity for affording such instruction in an effective manner. With their increase in wealth, religious observances have rapidly increased among the Free Settlers, and are daily spreading their healthy influence downwards, at little or no cost to the Mother Country.[clxxxiii]

William did not live to see his fears realized and died several years before the cessation came of Transportation. Interestingly as noted, Elizabeth Grey and her husband Frederick Innes became increasingly involved in the anti-slavery cause in England as well as the  anti-transportation movement in VDL. The tide of social evolution was  on their side   and eventually the flow of British prisoners to the island ceased.

This part of the story is about an Italian ring, Queen Elizabeth 1$^{st}$, her favoured courtier, a young Irish girl in Van Diemen's Land, the passion of young love, brucellosis and heart breaking loss. The tale begins at the end.

Little is known about young William Talbot except that he came from an ancient

Figure 14 Malahide VDL

Irish aristocratic lineage whose estates and castle were Malahide near Dublin. His family had lived there since the Twelfth Century. A relation of

young William, the Hon William Talbot, had been given a large land grant at Break-o-Day and he named it Malahide after his home in Ireland. The property still exists today and is owned by another branch of the family.

Mr Talbot is recorded as arriving in VDL on Friday June 1$^{st}$ 1832 and there is an entry with Mr Talbot leaving for Sydney on November 29$^{th}$ 1833. These dates fit well with the family story but his relationship with the Hon William or indeed any of the Talbot family remains a mystery. It has always been accepted that the Hon William was his uncle but Stephen Talbot, the family historian can find no trace of where William fits in their genealogy.

As we know William was never to return. He died of Neapolitan Fever (brucellosis) in Naples.[clxxxiv]

*But William was never to ride along that track again. At the time his ship was expected, his uncle found he was not on board. A passenger brought a letter.*

*He and his tutor were both at Naples, ill. They had Neapolitan fever. His grandfather and brother hurried post haste across Europe to get the best medical skill for them.*

Many months later the ring arrived and presented to Catherine.

*Not long after this letter, the ring came. Her parents made no remark when she put it on her engagement finger and was never seen without it until the end of her life.*

The ring itself is as beautiful as it is intriguing. It appears to be an earlier version of a Claddagh ring which became popular at the end of Elizabeth 1's reign. Named after the small fishing village of Claddagh on the West Coast of Ireland meaning flat stony shore.[clxxxv] Even today the village is still renowned for creating the ring. Varying myths and versions of its origin exist. However, its provenance dates is around 1596. Its central leitmotif is the intimacy of relationships.

"The Claddagh's distinctive design features two hands clasping a heart, usually surmounted by a crown. The elements of this symbol are often said to correspond to the qualities of love (the heart), friendship (the hands), and loyalty (the crown).[clxxxvi] The ring William was given for his future bride is simpler with two hands clasping, but no crown or heart. It resembles the more classical medieval 'fede motif' as described by the British Museum;

The fede motif (two clasped hands joined at the bezel) represents the joining of hands of the couple at a marriage ceremony, a practice that dates back to ancient Rome and was known as 'dextrarum iunctio'.[clxxxvii]

The ring also resembles a gimmel-ring popular at this time, evidenced in the Will of Johan Brouncker, who in 1577, left one 'Ringe of golde with an hande in hande' to her sister-in-law.[clxxxviii] One of two interlocking rings was given to the bride, the other to the bridegroom, and the rings were reunited at their wedding, and closely entwined with love, marriage and friendship. So the question is why would Queen Elizabeth 1st give such a gift to a 'Page' as indicated in Dougharty's description? A Page was usually a young boy of a well-known family at court.It seems more likely that she may have presented the ring to a favoured Courtier at a time of marriage. Politically the passing on such an intimate expression to an individual man seems improbable. A recipient of the ring could have been George Talbot, sixth Earl of Shrewsbury (c.1528 – 1590). While the Earl was not the most stimulating company he was solid, dependable and charged with the care of Mary Queen of Scots for nearly 15 years.

He clearly had a close relationship with the Queen which is borne out by the following;

in November (1568), the queen assured him that 'er it were longe he shuld well perseve she dyd so trust him as she dyd few." This assurance assumed a concrete form in December, on the 13th of which month Shrewsbury wrote to his wife, 'Now it is sarten the Scotes quene cumes to Tutburye to my charge.'[clxxxix]

This is also supported by her private letter during one of the most challenging times when she became scarred with smallpox.

The Queen to George Talbot, Earl of Shrewsbury, October 22 1572, informing him that she had had the smallpox, but is now recovered. A postscript in her own hand assures him that no one would know she had been ill: 'My faithfull Shrewesbury, Let no grief touche your harte for feare of my disease for I assure you if my creadit wer not greatar than my shewe, ther is no behooldar wold beleve that ever I had bin touched with such a maladye. Your faitheful

Lovinge Soveraine Elizabeth R.' (MS 3197, f.41)[cxc]


In 1568 George Talbot married Bess of Hardwick, an extremely rich and powerful widow who was also a confidante of the Queen.[cxci]Could that be when the ring was presented to the Talbot family? Clearly this may never be answered definitively. It should be noted the Earl's seat was in Sheffield rather than Malahide in Ireland although the families were connected and so the precise passage of the ring from Elizabethan England to VDL in 1833 may for-ever remain a mystery. Catherine Grey remained faithful to William and wore the ring for the rest of her life. She died on the 30th March 1902[cxcii]

GREY. — On Easter Day, March 30, at her residence, Brisbane-street, Launceston, Catherine, second daughter of the late Humphrey Grey, of Eastbourne, aged 85.

*The death is announced of Miss Grey, at Eastbourne, who*

*was known far and wide for her amiable qualities and [?] generosity. The deceased lady was one of the earliest colonists. Together with her father, Mr Humphrey Grey, and other members of her family, she experienced shipwreck when on her way out, and lived for twelve months in Rio Janeiro, and the good officers of the British Consul were bought into requisition and another ship called at the South American port, and carried the survivors to Hobart Town, at which place they arrived in 1829. Miss Grey was quite an authority on such matters respecting the early history of this State. She remembered when the blacks maintained a reign of terror, and she could recite the lawless acts of various bushrangers. Miss Grey being a neighbour of Mr John Batman when he lived at Kingsten, heard him describe the Port Phillip district in the most glowing terms, and she remembered Mr Batman carrying off the packing cases in which Major Grey's furniture can from England, with which he made a boat, that he might pass up the Yarra. It is not possible to chronicle her hosts of recollections, which were retained till quite recently.* cxciii

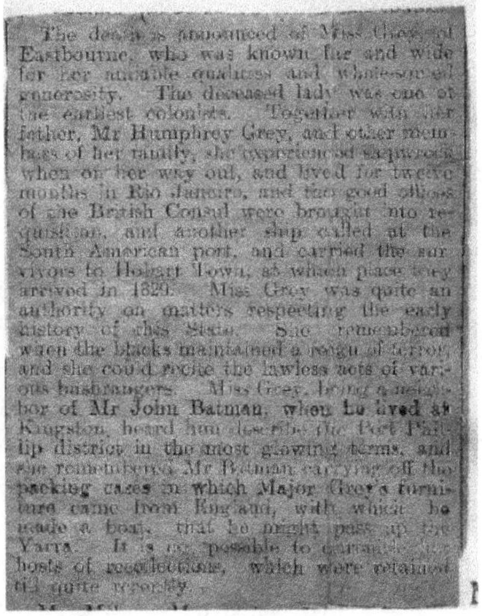
The [illegible] is announced of Miss Grey, of Eastbourne, who was known far and wide for her amiable qualities and [illegible] generosity. The deceased lady was one of the earliest colonists. Together with her father, Mr Humphrey Grey, and other members of her family, she experienced shipwreck when on her way out, and lived for twelve months in Rio Janeiro, and the good offices of the British Consul were brought into requisition, and another ship called at the South American port, and carried the survivors to Hobart Town, at which place they arrived in 1829. Miss Grey was quite an authority on matters respecting the early history of this State. She remembered when the blacks maintained a reign of terror, and she could recite the lawless acts of various bushrangers. Miss Grey, being a neighbor of Mr John Batman, when he lived at Kingston, heard him describe the Port Phillip district in the most glowing terms, and she remembered Mr Batman carrying off the packing cases in which Major Grey's furniture came from England, with which he made a boat, that he might pass up the Yarra. It is not possible to [illegible] her hosts of recollections, which were retained till quite recently.

Figure 15 Catherine Grey's Obitu-

# BOX FIFTEEN: BUILDING A CHURCH

The Gray family were Protestant and had a long history in Ireland dating back to the Cromwellian conquest. The family may have been Presbyterian as well as Church of Ireland at varying time but in VDL their allegiances were toward the Church of England, probably for practical reason of sharing their faith with a suitably sized congregation and thus securing a Minister.

A note from a Christian traveller in 1833 gives an insight into the character and values of the Gray family.

## Major Gray

1833. forming a striking object on the left, and the St. Paul's range bounding the view to the right. Major Grey's house is in the township of Avoca ; his brother, Captain Grey's, is not far distant, and is beautifully situated on the northern bank of the South Esk, We found Major Grey and his lady very intelligent and serious; the former is an active magistrate. They have a large family of young children who are a very promising group. Their excellent mother is a pattern both as regards her domestic duties and piety.

7th. J. Backhouse and myself returned to Major Grey's, and had some very interesting conversation with the Major and his wife. They have both lived to see the vanity of all earthly pursuits, and have been led to flee for refuge to the hope set before them in the Gospel, which hope they acknowledge to have felt as an anchor to the soul. The Major accompanied us to Ensign Adamson's cottage, where we spent a couple of hours in conversation, especially on the principles of the Temperance Society. Ensign Adamson declared his conviction that nineteen out of twenty of the offences for which the soldiery are punished, are the result of spirit-drinking: he said he had seriously thought of petitioning at head quarters, that the daily allowance of this pernicious beverage might be withdrawn.[cxciv]

Humphrey and his family were also steeped in tradition which helped them through troubled times. Amelia (Emily), his niece in Ireland sent him her father, Basil's (b1768) 'Book of Common Prayer,of the Church of England' dated 1712 Dated 1840.

My dearest Uncle Humphrey,

I also send you a prayer book, which my dear lamented father read with attention, made it his constant study and derived much benefit and comfort from. Interestingly there is a section at the back on the 'Martyrdom of King Charles I'. It should be remembered that while the Presbyterians and many others opposed the King they did not want him executed, a sentiment which was included in the Common Prayer Book. One reason also may have been that the book had to be approved by subsequent Kings and Queens.

Martyrdom of K.CHARLES.I.

Each family also suffered the loss of children accentuating their desire for a place to experience spiritual comfort and refection even faster. A church was planned, built and consecrated in Avoca amidst the most difficult of economic circumstances. The foundation stone for St Thomas' Anglican Church was laid by Governor Franklin in 1839

AVOCA The Lieutenant Governor visited Avoca on Saturday last in the course of his tour through the Colony he was received at the residences of Mr Talbot of Major and Captain Gray and spent between two and three days in the District. On Saturday His Excellency laid the foundation stone of a new church Episcopalian (Anglican) at Avoca when addresses were successively offered by the Arch Deacon and His Excellency.cxcv

Figure 16  View of Avoca, Tasmania, 1855, from a drawing by Emily Bowring.cxcvi

The Church was designed by James Blackburn who was responsible for many well-known churches and buildings in Tasmania. Build in the Romanesque Revival it was consecrated on 8 May 1842 by *Rev. Mr. Richardson who 'preached an appropriate sermon to a congregation of about one hundred and twenty persons: after service the sacrament was administered.'*cxcvii The building had cost nearly £1800;

£700 was granted by government, and the balance evidences the liberality of the inhabitants of the district, who have not only found funds for the completion of the church, but have also generously contributed towards the erection of a parsonage house, which will be finished in about nine months.

The main contributors were three wealthy men in the district: Mr Simeon Lord, Humphrey Grey and William Gray. **The families were also very much involved with** the development of the district and active in written petitions to the government in relation to improvement of roads, the need for a bridge and even their concern for Christian education.[cxcviii]

**Figure 17 Humphrey Grey b1780 died in Tasmania**

*"Mr Grey together with Messrs. Siemon Lord and Major Grey, made possible the building of this Church by becoming guarantors in 1838 to the Government according to the Church Act of 1837. He arrived with his family in Van Diemen's Land in 1828. He was previously in the Imperial Commisariat Dept. on the side of Loyalty in the Irish Rebellion of 1798. On arrival Settled in the Avoca Dist. where he resided for over 40 years, He died at the age of 88 years. Great Industry & Probity brought affluence & respect. Of unobstrusive habits, great intelligence, warm hospitality, he made friends with all he came in contact with."*

The final service at St Thomas' Anglican Church was held on 23rd June 2019 after 180 years of service to the community

# BOX SIXTEEN: FAMILY DYNAMICS, ELLENTHORPE

Like all families there were constant changes as children grew through different phases of life. By the early 1830s Henrietta was old enough to go to boarding school and later joined by her sister Lysbeth. This was also a practical move to remove her from the dangers of their situation and the fact that they did not yet have a proper house to live in may also have influenced this decision.

Their journey by bullock would have been at a gentle pace, through picturesque countryside, the tranquility although most probably was punctuated by language unfamiliar to young ladies, by the Bullockee. They had armed riders for protection and the journey would have taken days.

One traveler, Augusta Prinsep, in 1830 observed such a party;

At Mr Harrison's we met another party of travellers, who were conveying a young lady to a famous boarding-school, about five miles off, kept by a Mrs. Clark. Who would have thought of finding such and establishment in the bush![cxcix]

They was sent to Ellinthorpe Hall run by a delightfully eccentric woman Mrs George Clark, formally Hannah Maria Davice, in their home just outside Ross.[cc] She must have seemed enchanting and a little mysterious to her young charge, with her large, dark eyes and black curly hair indicative of her Spanish heritage. Mr Clark was equally intriguing with only one eye as a result of an errant arrow released by a younger brother. He was affectionately known as 'Old One Eye' although it is doubtful the pupils would have been so bold to have addressed him thus.

The school had been running for several years before Henrietta joined to be educated in the following areas:

The Pupils are Educated in every branch of Female Acquirement usually taught in the first Schools in England, comprising especially the English and French Languages (in .. which the principles of general Grammar Are carefully imparted). Writing and Arithmetic, Geography; usefully and ornamental Needle Work; Music Drawinging & Dancing. (Colonial Times 1827)[cci]

In addition to formal education 'Every attention would be paid to deportment and they would be practiced in the usage of polite society'.

The cost of her boarding at the time was £40 pa with an additional £20 for pupils who took all the extra subjects.

Although the Greys sent the girls there as much for protection as education it was far from safe. For the first few years a military post was established close to the Hall to protect the school against attacks by both Aborigines and Bushrangers. Once a month the officers were invited to Ellinthorpe to spend the evening at the school where the older girls would take it in turns to act as hostess. However, a few year later in 1838 they were all in peril from Bushrangers.

Figure 18 Ellenthorpe Hall near Ross H.G. Lloyd, Creator: Lloyd, Henry Grant, 1830-1904 Allport Library and Museum of Fine Arts

On the 3<sup>rd</sup> May three escaped convicts Palmer, Regan and Thomas, who were well known to locals through their attacks and murder across the Midlands, arrived at Ellinthorpe at about 11.30am and took several servants as hostages. Mr Clark, ever the gentleman, took it upon himself to see the girls safely to an upstairs room whereupon 'instead of leading his men secluded himself in his bedroom!'.[ccii] In the meantime downstairs, the siege continued until John Ward, an assigned convict, shot and killed Palmer. Regan the leader was later heard to remark with some irony that it would save the trouble of him being hanged. They left calmly with four hostages and all the valuables they could carry to their horses, released the men and quickly disappeared. It is suggested that Mrs Clark, never to miss aneducational opportunity, led all the teachers and girls past Palmer's and being 'a devotee of the science of phrenology, is said even to have examined the bumps of Palmer's head'.[cciii] The bushrangers were soon captured, the heroic convicts given their freedom and Mr Clark's reputation somewhat tarnished!

Lysbeth appeared to have gained a sound education from her years at Ellinthorpe. This is evidenced in a letter she wrote from St Helena in 1841 when she would have been about 20 years old. Standing at the original grave of Napoleon she wrote:

I am much more sensibly affected by the spectacle of a ruined city with its broken arches and columns, its desolate and moss- grown temples; by the spectacle which exhibits the supremacy of that providence which <u>casts down</u> as much as raises up; - Pompeii, or Carthage in the ruins among which Marius was taken; Charles the fifth reduced to a trembling superstitious monk; or Napoleon with only the memories of fugitive majesty and Dominion; - than I ever am by any spectacle of existing pomp or power. In the latter it is only our vulgar taste for the dazzling which is gratified; but in the former our moral & imaginative nature finds a subduing yet a dignified theme. Here I stood upon ground often prepared by him who was the author & thrower down of imperial dynasties – from which <u>he </u>had often viewed the same congenial prospect of the restless and immeasurable ocean. [The complete letter may be found in Appendix A]

Clearly an intelligent, articulate letter with an insight based on her depth of knowledge of European history and culture. Lysbeth was well regarded throughout her life for her intellect and her thoughtful discourse. Her later home at Newlands it is said was full of books and literature in many areas of human scholarship.

# BOX SEVENTEEN: CHANGING TIMES 1840 - 1849

The families' fortunes and material serenity was greatly disturbed by the economic depression of the period. The whole of VDL was affected by the late 1830s recession in England resulting in lower wool prices and the collapse of the food and grain markets to NSW. Capital was draining from VDL to the new colony of Port Phillip and the Government was in severe debt. The advent of new taxes, the ever increasing costs of the convict system caused disruption and division between the Lt-Governor Eardley-Wilmot and the Legislative Council. Several members of the Legislative Council resigned in protest.

Goods remained unsold on the shelves of local shops, unemployment was chronic, with free settlers competing for jobs with ticket-of leave convicts.

Bankruptcies by 1843 involved not only town business but farms and land owners as well. Two banks closed. The society itself was changing too. Many citizens had now been born in VDL and were growing up in a country alien and distant from Mother England which they still called 'Home'. With rapidly rising population others were tiring of the military, convict culture and the often bungling bureaucratic powers and idiosyncrasies of the Governor of the day.

Two forces for change were beginning to take hold: the first to stop transportation and the second for greater independence from the direct control from Westminster. In other words the desire for a democratically elected form of government, though only for wealthy men of course! The former was abhorrent to the Gray brothers. They had also petitioned for retention of Transportation in the late 1830s after a Parliamentary enquiry in England had raised many social and economic concerns in relation to the penal system in VDL.

However as the economy slumped so too did employment levels. The situation was now dramatically different from the frontier days of the colony when convict labour was used for all manner of assignments, including building infrastructure, clearing land, working as servants and so on. Now there was an abundance of people wanting work so convict labour was seen to be taking work from those who were free and needed to be paid to support their families. Not only that but to add insult the 'Home' government and the Governor were now seeking to tax the colony in order to pay for some of the costs associated with keeping the convicts, a move fiercely and successfully fought.

For a conservative, establishment family such movements and shifts in social values would have been an anathema. Major Gray, stiff and uncompromising, whose power and authority had been unquestioned for so long would go on fighting for the status quo for the rest of his life. James probably agreed with his older brother while Humphrey may have been more comfortable with some of the new ideas. His new son-in-law, Frederick Innes, and his daughter Lysbeth, clearly, held more libertarian views.

In this context of significant economic and social upheaval the three families survived in different ways with a range of different outcomes, although their focus during the early 1840s years appears to have been on things more ecclesiastical, in the form of building a Church the machinations of which was covered earlier.

## Death of William

William maintained his magistrate's and Justice of the Peace's duties as well as overseeing Rockford. Although he survived the depression and even managed to donate a considerable sum to the Church his financial situation would, like many others have been quite straitened. Most certainly the value of his property plummeted during this decade. Even so the 1847 census revealed that he had 21 people in his household, eleven of whom were free and the remainder bonded. Unbeknown to them this would be the last New Year's Eve celebrations they were to spend together as a family. Within a few weeks the pressure of work coupled with perhaps an edgy temperament led to William's having a stroke and dying on the 10th March 1848, at the age of 55.[cciv] His adoring brother James signed the death certificate as the Deputy Registrar at Avoca.

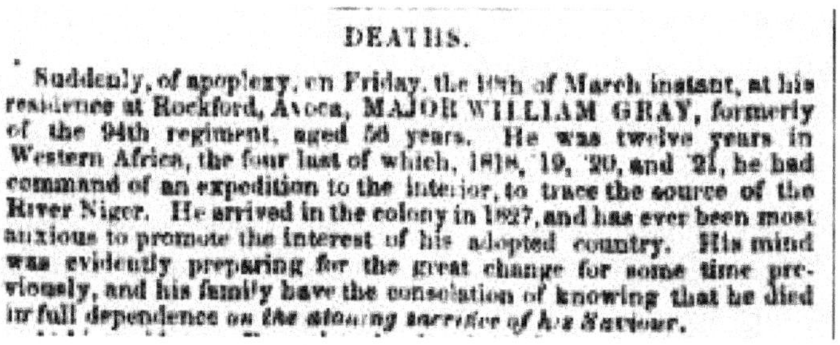

### DEATHS.

Suddenly, of apoplexy, on Friday, the 10th of March instant, at his residence at Rockford, Avoca, MAJOR WILLIAM GRAY, formerly of the 94th regiment, aged 56 years. He was twelve years in Western Africa, the four last of which, 1818, '19, '20, and '21, he had command of an expedition to the interior, to trace the source of the River Niger. He arrived in the colony in 1827, and has ever been most anxious to promote the interest of his adopted country. His mind was evidently preparing for the great change for some time previously, and his family have the consolation of knowing that he died in full dependence on the atoning sacrifice of his Saviour.

Figure 19 William Gray's death notice Courier 18th March

*Suddenly, of apoplexy, on Friday, the 10th of March instant, at his residence at Rockford, Avoca,*

*MAJOR WILLIAM GRAY, formerly of the 94th regiment, aged 56 years. He was twelve years in Western Africa, the four last of which, 1818, '19, '20, and '21, he had command of an expedition to the interior, to trace the source of the River Niger. He arrived in the colony in 1827, and has ever been most anxious to promote the interest of his adopted country. His mind was evidently preparing for the great change for some time previously, and his family have the consolation of knowing that he died full dependence on the atoning sacrifice of his Saviour.*

William's Will provided fewsurprises except for the seemingly low valuation of his estate at £300. It left Elleanor with little to support her children although sufficient to allow her to stay at Rockford for several more years. During this time Elleanor's daughter Fanny Anne Talbot married Alexander Thompson at Avoca on 17th March 1853.[ccv] Eventually Elleanor moved to Melbourne to be with her son Basil. She died on the 28th December 1869 aged 79. It is interesting reflection to read her death notice which says far more about her husband William, than Eleanor herself. She was the last surviving member of her generation.

*GRAY. — On the 28th inst., at Whithyfield, Brunswick, the residence of her son Basil Gray, in the 79th year of her   age,*

Eleanor  Toler  Gray, relict of Major William Gray, of Rockford, Avoca, Tasmania, and of Her Majesty's 94th Regiment, commander of the Military Exploration of Africa, on the river Niger, in 1816. Tasmanian and Dublin.[ccvi]

### Death of James

The Grayfort clan began the decade with the hope and joy engendered by the birth of a son Richard Talbot on 27th May 1842. However the celebrations were to be short lived for James and his family. James was a far more carefree character than either his brother or cousin. Although the 1830s had been prosperous and in many respects relatively easy to succeed with good wool prices and a steady market for grain, the real test for any farmer is when the leaner periods take hold. James perhaps had a temperament far more suited to prosperity than leaner times.

The Depression of the early 1840s hit many people very hard. Bankruptcies spread through all sectors of society. While it is one thing to be given land, free or cheap labour, it is quite another for an ex-army officer to learn the skills required to be a successful long term farmer. Such a sentiment was also expressed by the Land Commissioner as earlier as 1828 when he observed so many neglected and poorly run farms.

The old saying, "Ne sutor ultra crepidum" ("Let the cobbler stick to his last")is very applicable to many who arrive here as Settlers. A regular apprenticeship must be served to every trade and profession but that of Famer. No matter what line of life a Man has followed at home, he imagines that he can farm to advantage in Van Diemen's Land. He sets out in quest of land, he pitches upon a spot that is evident to all acquainted with the matter must be his ruin, but, he fancies himself wiser than all who have come before him, nor will he take any advice, supposing that it is given from selfish and interested  motives.[ccvii]

The wise words of Mr. Micawber to young David Copperfield yet to be written by Charles Dickens, would have saved James a great deal of misery.

Annual income twenty pounds, annual expenditure nineteen nineteen six, result happiness. Annual income twenty pounds, annual expenditure twenty pounds ought and six, result misery.[ccviii]

James certainly tried to improve his circumstance by becoming the postmaster at St Paul's Plains from 1 June 1832 to 1 April 1835 and took on the responsibility for the postal run from Campbell Town along the Fingal Valley for the princely sum of £200

**GENERAL POST OFFICE.**
*26th August, 1841.*

It is hereby notified for the information of the parties concerned, and the public generally, that the following Tenders for the conveyance of certain Branch Mails, for two years, from the 1st October next, have been accepted :—

To and from Campbell Town, Avoca, and St. Patrick's Head, James K. Gray, £200 per annum.

pa.[ccix] James also reduced his household staff  significantly from 12 in the 1843 census to three by 1848. However by  1843 even this was not enough to pay James' outstanding account at Jordon's Tailor in Launceston and he was forced to sell part of his land. It should be remembered that city merchants were the first to be affected by the economic downturn and hence the need to take somewhat drastic and unpopular action.

At one stage, Humphrey helped by purchasing some of his land but in the end by November 1847 James Kinsley Gray was declared Bankrupt.[ccx] The notice reads in part; 'In the matter of insolvency of James Kingsley Gray, of Avoca, in Van Diemen's Land, Farmer.' … 'An application for an order of charge of the said insolvent'

The last few years of James' life had been hard. He had lost his son James, their baby Ellen, he was bankrupt, still supporting a large household at Grayfort and his ever present, adored, older brother William had recently died. The toll took its course and as in life James followed his brother in death. James Kinsley Gray died of a heart attack on the 18th May 1849 at Grayfort. Mary was left with a family to support and the responsibility of paying off any remaining debts. More land was sold soon after James' death. However Mary still managed to retain some land and was listed as a lessor and landlady in 1856. Clearly she was more adept at financial management than her late husband! During this time Mary faced yet another heart-break, alone, with the death from consumption (TB) of Mary Ellen, her third daughter, at 23 years of age.

On the 5th instant, of consumption, Mary Ellen, third daughter of the late Lieut. James Kingsley Gray, of Grayfort, aged 23 years.[ccxi] Eventually Mary moved to Melbourne to be closer to her family. She died on the 9th October 1865 aged 63 years.

On the 9th October, at her residence, Alma-terrace, St. Kilda, Mary Gray, widow of the late Lieut. James K. Gray, of Gray Fort, Avoca, Tasmania, aged sixty-three years.[ccxii]

# BOX NINETEEN: SHIPS AND SOCIAL LIFE RETURN TO STORY

### The Flying Squadron

This was a time of extraordinary change for the Royal Navy. The future was now clear, sail would soon be a relic of history as steam power and metal took pride of place in the design of British warships. Even with the disastrous sinking of the Captain there would be no turning back and in 1873 the HMS *Devastation* was launched, the first ever steam-only battleship and proved to be a powerful weapon in the British Fleet. Added to this, Gladstone, the Prime Minister, had embarked on a program of social reform which required funds, resulting in the reduction of the Navy from 17000 to 10000 men.

Perhaps by way of consolation the Lords of the Admiralty organised an around-the-World tour of the Colonies and other nations in 1869. The purpose was to maintain the prestige of wooden boats, show the Flag, and for the furtherance and instruction of seamanship although in reality it seems to have been a voyage of pleasure.[ccxiii]

Hence to the surprise and delight of the people of Hobart on the 2nd January 1870 they looked out to see the spectacle of Royal Navy ships sailing into the Derwent estuary. They were to see the flag ship, the Liverpool and then the Liffy, Bristol, Endymion, Scylla, Barrosa, Phoebe, Charybdis, and the Satelite.[ccxiv]

The view from a seaman's point of view was no less enticing. Marcus McCausland, a midshipman on board the frigate HMS *Liffey*, in his diary. The Cruise of The Flying Squadron 1869 – 1870;

Sunday Jan 2nd Arrived off Hobart Town. Crowds of people down by the water side watching us come in. In fact the churches were empty and they say the Bishop cut his sermon short by saying, "Dearly beloved brethren, the Flying Squadron are coming in and I must be off to see them". I watched the Admiral as he landed and saw him surrounded by women. A sailor's interests and extra curricula activities are timeless, if not predictable;

We acted a second time before the Governor The Honourable

Mr DuCann and Lady DuCann, Admiral Hornby and all the elite of Hobart town. The proceeds of the performance went to the organ fund the members of which stood us a great supper at the Bird in Hand Public House after which we paraded the streets during the night singing squadron songs. I then retired to my hotel and spent the remainder of the night with a mess- mate in trying to enter the landlady's room, where the poor unprotected female slept with two pretty barmaids. We wrenched the alarm bell off her door and then got in through the window but cowardly wretches as we were, we were beaten off by her ladyship a big stick in one hand and a jug of water in the other - and she only in her nightgown. We kept the attack up till daylight and then had to desist.[ccxv]

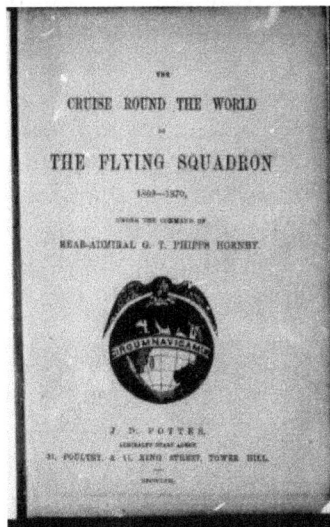

The official version of the Flying Squadron was written by Rear- Admiral G. T Phipps Hornby and is a detailed log of the trip. It is freely available online. Flying Squadron, 1869-1870 under the command of Rear-Admiral G.T. Phipps Hornby [compiled by J.B. and Henry Cavendish].Published 1871.

Hornby's account though reads more like a gossipy magazine than an a official account of a Royal Navy tour including somewhat disparaging comments about the beauties of Hobart.

As we had heard on constant cry in Australia about the beauty of Tasmanian women of "Wait till you go to Hobarton," we waited; and as the day drew near, anxiety increased to see the room which was to be full of dazzling visions, and like most other things in this life that you look forward to with interest, we hope it will not be considered heresy to say that we were a little disappointed as to the amount of beauty in it. That there were pretty girls in undeniable, but that they were very scarce we think equally so. What nature had not lavished, artifice had usurped the place with little winning ways. And many hearts beat a shade quicker as the sight of a well- remembered Melbourne face.[ccxvi]

Needless to say not everyone was pleased with the book, as witnessed in an outraged letter to the Editor[ccxvii];

## THE CRUISE OF THE FLYING SQUADRON:TO THE EDITOR OF THE MERCURY.

Sir,-I have to thank you for your review of the above publication in last Tuesday's Mercury, ....... I may esteem it a providential event-in carrying out my intention, and thereby innocently introducing into a young family a book so demoralising and disgusting, and, as a literary production, beneath contempt. I felt as if I had escaped some loathsome pitfall concealed beneath the laurels and the time-honoured flag of the British navy.

In times past when such men-of-war us the Pelorus, Erebus, Terror, &c., visited our shores, the officers were valiant seamen, true gentlemen, and with few exceptions accomplished scholars. They were treated with the hospitality proverbial in Tasmania, and the ladies of the colony received from these gentlemen the attention and respect due to their sex.

A few years later, and the daughters of these ladies are shamefully traduced, and held up to the scorn of the world by men who have been, as their predecessor were, received with kindness and treated with hospitality; but they, in return, have endeavoured to destroy the fair fame, not only of the daughters of Tasmania, but of every colony they have blasted with their presence. All are alike branded in this book as women scarcely a remove from "La Traviata," with details coarse and disgusting, and insinuations demoralising.

We trust the friends in England of Viscountess Canterbury and Lady Belmore, whose feelings have been so wantonly outraged, and hospitality so shamefully abused, will call the attention of the Lords of the Admiralty to a production that will raise the just indignation and disgust of the Australian colonies, and is also calculated to affect the honour of the British navy. Did the author of the "Cruise"act on the same principle, and hope to make their work acceptable lo a certain class by hashing up such unsavoury and immodest details, and dragging in the names and initials of ladies? Shame on any man who could so forget his manhood...

The authors of these base libels may expect that the gold reaped by such cowardly and unmanly detraction will be rusted and turned to ashes by the scorn of the wives and daughters of the Australias.

There is also mention by Hornby of hospitality which may well have been at Newlands, the Innes home in Newtown.[ccxviii]

Regardless of Hornby's condescension it was certainly a week to be remembered by a small, sleepy town in the far flung corner of the Empire although if Marcus and companions did have their way its population may well have been augmented a little later in the year.

---

Sunday, January 9th.—In the morning the ships were crowded with visitors of all classes of the community, to enjoy the novelty of ship and short service. The vice-regal party went on board the " Liverpool," and the head of the Tasmanian Church preached on board the " Endymion."   The afternoon was devoted

to tender partings of a very non-ordinary order, all Hobart Town and the surrounding country being largely sprinkled with weeping men and wailing women, the hospitable house of beauty at New Town becoming temporarily a house of woe, the heaviest sufferers being those that recklessly stayed for evening service, tea, etc., and finishing almost fatally with poor mamma going to bed with such a headache.   In

**Written by Sarah Elizabeth Innes (Grey)**

A voyage of about two months duration from the Australian shores bought us within the welcome sight of the first land which relieved the blue monotony of our prospect, on the morning of April 8th 1841. Going upon dusk, at about a quarter past six o'clock, I saw an immense rock, which with the deception common to objects at sea, appeared close to us in a north – easterly direction. This was St Helena, a spot familiar to my imagination & my thoughts from its connection with perhaps the most wonderful mortal who has trodden our earth. The Island presented a bare, rugged, aspect. The only indications of verdure in occasional vallies,[1] which came under our notice in the vessels track to a safe anchorage.

James' Town, the capital of St Helena, is situated in one of these vallies, & is encompassed by precipitous hills: vessels anchor close to it in the only situation from which the town can be seen at any distance. There were several there at this time, whalers, and a Queens brig employed on the African coast on the look-out for slavers. Four slave-ships had been captured & bought to St Helena just before we put in there. I met a Portuguese Captain who had repeatedly been taken when engaged in the diabolical traffic.

The man's countenance accorded with the character for his occupation. A pair of black & grey eye-brows [unreadable word], but did not obscure eyes whose 'laughing Devil' expression, spoke cunning, contempt, & ferociousness; he was little, & had the worn appearance of age without however any indication of its feebleness. There might be some prejudice in my estimate of the human form before me, because it was that of a dealer in his fellow creatures; but it did remind me of the Satanic; it chilled & disgusted me. The slave captain seemed to me a being incapable of possessing or commanding love or confidence. Our feeling in an empire of freemen, under a government in which a slave cannot breathe, is to who has been a slave finds his fetters[2] taken off, have been so much taxed for the last twenty years or more by accounts of slavery, & further horrors of the slave-trade, that aversion to these foul stains in the pages of human history, has ceased to do so much as passim[3] as a principle; has ceased to be justified so much by reason for humanity as by those of political expediency; and while this principle is active & efficient in its operation, it may not be questioned that many secret suspicions are entertained that the accounts which have been given of slavery & the slave trade, have been rather over-charged, for the sake of effect.

At least I must frankly allow that for some time I entertained such suspicions. But let such as think that this traffic has been pictured by Wilberforce & now Clarksons in character of exaggeration go on board a slave-ship & they will be undeceived. As I have said before some of these tubs – for they are little better, - had been captured a short time previously; and three of them lay not far from our anchorage. They looked like so many dingy, very inferior, coal boats; and when out at sea can have none of the majesty of a ship in sail. These vessels are, I was informed, generally broken up & sold in a state of dismemberment at St. Helena.

[1] Vallies obsolete spelling for Valleys

2 Fetters: a chain or shackle fastened to somebody's ankles or feet. (Encarta Dictionary English UK sighted 3/Sept 15) 3 Passim: throughout, frequently, everywhere (Word synonyms)

The negroes were in quarantine in another part of the island where we found them merry & careless as the negro generally is; excepting those who had been most recently landed many of whom were sickly, & some apparently in an almost hopeless state. Our enquiring their future destination I was informed that on a certificate of their restoration to health being given by the Medical Superintendent, they would be appreciated on the island. Hard is the lot of these poor victims of the white, the "civilised" man's selfish avarice! Their only protection from the chain & the last entailing the annihilation of the relationship with its happy sympathetic & affections, of parent, son, or brother! They are exiles in the most heart-touching sense of the word; exiles not from senseless earth merely, but from Domestic loves!

There are some good houses, & places of public, built of stone at St Helena. Most of the houses & other buildings have flat roofs covered with earth & gravel, which fall in frequently after heavy rains. James Town has a very irregular appearance; the streets are so narrow that I do not think two gigs could pass each other; and they are also very steep. We procured a four wheeled machine, the best that was not already engaged, the reluctant progress of which, drawn as it was by one horse, was assisted by runners/men who live by that employment/ and proceeded to Longwood,4 which is situated at about seven miles from the Harbour. It was on continued ascent the entire way until we reached Longwood, where the country presented an unexpected & very fertile appearance. From this elevation a fine prospect was afforded us of the harbour, and of the sea-coast girding the island, for some miles around. At our right stood the house which sheltered the last days, received the last breath, of the fallen Bonaparte. I cannot well describe my feelings in contemplating so interesting and striking a memorial of human greatness passed away. I am much more sensibly affected by the spectacle of a ruined city with its broken arches and columns, its desolate and moss-grown temples; by the spectacle which exhibits the supremacy of that providence which casts down as much as raises up; - Pompeii, or Carthage in the ruins among which Marius was taken; Charles the fifth reduced to a trembling superstitious monk; or Napoleon with only the memories of fugitive majesty and Dominion; - than I ever am by any spectacle of existing pomp or power. In the latter it is only our vulgar taste for the dazzling which is gratified; but in the former our moral & imaginative nature finds a subduing yet a dignified theme. Here I stood upon ground often prepared by him who was the author & thrower down of imperial dynasties – from which he had

Figure 20 Longwood was Napoleon's residence on Saint Helena from 1815 until his death six years later. (Public domain)

often viewed the same congenial prospect of the restless and immeasurable ocean. Every step I took, every object which presented itself bought in man's character before my mind the regal prisoner of St Helena. The house inhabited by Napoleon reminds the English visitor of some decayed farm-house. It is now held by Mr Mason, who has converted it into a barn and stables. So much for Mr Mason's good taste, & delicacy of sentiment. In the very room, in which, surrounded by the scanty number of his faithful attendants, the Emperor firmed his mortality. I found standing a thrashing machine; in this same room.

I was left to conclude, it was usually employed. A book is kept in which visitors enter their names with occasionally brief remarks upon the place & I could not fail to sympathise in the indignant expressions which I found attached to the signatures, chiefly of French visitors, at the mean purposes to which the spot marked by so interesting a history, was condemned without any great admiration for Napoleon, or respect for his character, - I say that I sympathise in the expressions recorded. In reference to Napoleon, or his character, it is of little moment, whether a palace or a dung-pile might be made of his last living abode.

But in reference to French feelings the case is different, it is more than needless to outrage them. And, in there not a fund of moral interest & instruction in the places associated with what is great or remarkable, in social or individual history which is at best sacrificed, in any case for a paltry and unequal return! We erect monuments at much cost of genius, of capital & industry, to commemorate events, that are never so well commemorated by those means, as by a tree, a stone, or house which had a contemporaneous existence & use in connection with the merits that we would not have drop into oblivion. There is a spiritual reality; a speaking, breathing power in the one memorial, which is wanting in the other.

The charge for admittance to the house was 3/6. The Prince de Joinville[5] when he visited St Helena for the purpose of removing Napoleon's remains expressed it as his intention to recommend to his father – Louis Philippe – to pension the persons who show the place to strangers, by way of recompensing them for the loss, which it was anticipated, they would encounter in the diminution of visitors after the exhumation.

We returned toward James Town by much the same direction as our party had come, - passing out of the way however to visit the grave of Napoleon. The grave is situated in a beautiful valley about three miles from James' Town; we did not wonder that it was the favourite walk for the Emperor; for here about there was a placid stillness which invited to a lonely [unreadable word]; & rendered it the most fitting spot also for the last resting place of mortal flesh. – By a strange fatuity we cannot help thinking sometimes as we contemplate a quiet country churchyard, or on the other hand, one in a noisy bustling thoroughfare, in a crowded city, that the first is fit and suitable, the other liable to prove different; forgetting that the silence of the grave cannot be, either broken, or made more silent! Everything in human hands is converted to traffic, to profit; - must be paid for if it be desired; and 3/6 was again demanded of me – for seeing the Emperor's <u>forsaken</u> grave. By the way, speaking of its being <u>forsaken</u>, on every side of the grave I found marks of French enthusiasm in reference to the idol of that people. Trees, shrubs, stones, everything at all in the locality of Napoleon's burial place seemed to have been wrested away, to be preserved as mementos. The famous

[5] François d'Orléans, Prince of Joinville willow was leafless, branchless, altogether gone.[6] The very earth which encompassed his body was visibly diminished – taken away. The top or headstone, a great part of the iron railing, had preceded other, less striking, memorials in falling into the hands of relic seekers.

Our guide had been on the island in the life-time of the spirit of the place, and he spoke with the anecdote of a familiar, & the pride of one who wants to boast having seen more that his listening visitors could pretend to. He was an old English Sargent, & could this tell us as he did even more liberally than we desired of Napoleon in his wars as well as his exile. But his fluency amounted to warmth when he touched upon the removal of the

Emperor's remains and upon the havoc the French had committed in their visit to the island for that purpose; I thought the old man's vehemence not quite disinterested as he spoke upon the topic. The diminution of interest in the spot & of visitors with their solid cash seemed to pass before his eyes!

The well from which Napoleon used to drink was close by the grave; it was sheltered by a hedge, & the water was, I thought – I do not know whether association & fatigue influenced my opinion – delicious, - such as I had never taken before.

My time being limited I hurried back to James' Town & on board ship again, having possessed myself of some Napoleon relics which are now more abundant than genuine I fear at St Helena; every body pretending to have them & pressing them upon for purchase. I spent a happy day, & laid in store a fund of observations with beguile the remaining weeks of our passage to England. S.E.I. (Sarah Elizabeth Innes)

Ccxix Napoleon's tomb St Helena 1833 from a watercolour by Lt H Jervis

# Appendix B: Grey Family Tree

**Sir William Caulfeild 2nd Baron Charlemont 1587-1640 = Mary King Lady Charlemont 1600-1663**

Children:
- Capt. Robert Caulfeild 4th Baron Charlemont 1622-AD 1643/44
- Hon. Anne Caulfeild Lady Wroth 1623-1682
- Col the Rt-Hon. William Caulfeild 1st Viscount Charlemont 1624-1671
- Mary Caulfeild 1625-1668
- George Caulfeild 1629-1658
- Capt. Thomas Caulfeild 1631-AD 1690/91
- John Caulfeild 1632-1676
- Margaret Caulfeild Lany Acheson 1633-1685

**Mary Caulfeild 1625 - 24 Jan 1668 = William Basil d 1693**

- Martin Caulfeild Basil d1735
- Mary Basil
- Edmund Basil
- Anne Basil
- Hannah = W George Harpur of Ballyfinn, Queens
- Elizabeth M Gilbert Graves of Stradbally, Queens

Mr Henry Grey of Kinsale Uncle to John Grey

Col Henry Grey brother to John Grey died in Irish Campaign

Three sisters to John Grey

Several daughters

**Colonel John Gray = Mary Basil**

John = ?

Basil b circa 1704 = Elizabeth, daughter of Captain W Carr.

John = Miss Rae, Castle Mitchell, County Kildare

Issue: Basil, Humphrey, Hannah, Sarah. No further mention of these

Basil, Surveyor of Excise, Coleraine. Unmarried d 1825 aged 63

Richard MD = Anne Kingsley b1760 d 25/4/1837 lived at Birr (Parsonstown), Kings Co.

William b 1732 of Garry Castle, Galway = Anne, daughter of R Wood

Humphrey b1744 = Anne Cluxton (First Marriage in 1766) Second Marriage = Sarah French

John b1746 = Hannah Fawcett, Garrymecas, Queens on 21 April 1775

Other chilren - William died young; Humphrey lived in Galway, Mary = Lt Abbott; Elizabeth = George Taylor of Cumber; Anne = Seargants

French Captain 1st Ceylon M Ursula Mooyart, niece of the Governor of Ceylon

Children from first marriage: Basil b 4th Jan 1768 at Roscomroe; Eliza died young; Margaret 1770 - 1787 aged 17

**\* Humphrey 1880 - 4th May 1868 = Catherine Mahony 1779 - 5th Nov 1847 of Mallow, Co Cork on Feb 1806**

Other Children: Elizabeth = George Kingston of Fermony Co Cork; Warburton Capt 56th Reg = Rose Adams; William Capt 58th Reg M = Sophia Bloomfield; Richard Capt 1st Ceylon = Anne Cavendish

Basil Fawcett John Rebeca Nicholas

William Basil George Eliza = Joseph Broomfield

**\* James d 18/5/1849 = Mary Legge 1802 - 23 Oct 1865**

Richard MD lived at Nenagh, Tipperary

Basil, Ensign Royal African Corp d unmarried

Margaret Helena 1807 22 December 1860 = Daniel R Falkiner

Humphrey William 1809 - 1836

Sarah Anne Grey Baptised 2nd Oct 1810 Mallow, Cork, Ireland Died young

Catherine (Kate) 1816 - 30 Mar 1902

Henrietta Emily 1820 - 28th June 1899 = John Thompson 1819 - 12 June 1899

Sarah Elizabeth (Lysbeth) 1821 - 4 Sept 1897 = Frederick Maitland Innes

**\* William 14 Mar 1793 - 10 March 1848 = Eleanor Toler Kingsley 1790 - 28/12/1869**

Richard 1823 in Ireland - 28 Nov 1839 aged 16 Avoca; William Kingsley Gray born in Ireland d 10/1/1866 Bungrutrong NSW; Humphrey Arthur 1827 in VDL - 15/4/1882; Basil 3 Oct 1829; Toler b 15th Feb 1834 (lost at sea); Gray, Robert James b 18 Feb 1841

Blanche Eliza 1826 - Aug 1911; Anna Frances 13 Sept 1827 - 5 July 1873 = Alfred Darby; James Vincent 15 Nov 1828 - 15 Nov 1838; Mary Eliza 29 Jan 1831 - 5th Dec 1853; Elizabeth b 14th Feb 1832 = William Alexander Jennings; William Legge b 2rd or 5th Nov 1833; Ellen Gray 1 Feb 1839 - 18th March 1839; Richard Talbot 27th May 1842 - 7th April 1875

Alice Kate = John Robertson; Humphrey Richard = Marian O'Connor, John William unmarried

Emily
Alexander John d 18 April 1875 aged 21
Catherine d 19th Oct 1927
Lavington Grey MD d 24th Oct 1923
Margaret d about 20 years old
Elizabeth Alice = ? Mackay of Kinlochberrie, Scotland in 1887
Ada died about 20 years old

(Text taken from Lysbeth's Bible 1825)

**Humphrey William Grey Innes** born at 13 Millman Street Bedford Mews London, 20th April 1842; ¼ past 3 AM

**Fredrick Maitland Inness** Born at Holyrood Street Newport, Isle of Wight 11 June 1843 at 10 minutes from 6pm.

**Catherine Henrietta Inness** Born at Newtown Hobart V D Land 19th November 1844 at ¼ to 5 AM

**Elizabeth Francis Inness** Born at Newtown Road Hobart Tasmania 16th May 1846 ¼ to 1 AM

**John Henry Innes** born at Lyttleton St Launceston Tasmania October 23rd 1867

**Mervyn Frank Innes** Born at ? Patterson's Plains. Tasmania 18 June 1849

**Margaret Maria Innes** Born at Woodmount Evandale 8 July 1851 ten minutes to ten PM

**Sydney Evelyn Innes** Born at ? street Launceston 26 June 1853

**Robert Russell Innes** Born at Woodmount. Evandale 27th June 1857

**Warburton Grey Innes** Born April 26th 1859 at Cottage Green Hampten Road Hobart Town

**Mary Louisa Isabelle** Born 17th September ¼ to 11 am 1862 At Newlands Newtown

## Appendix B: Grey Family Tree

\* families who emigrated to VDL

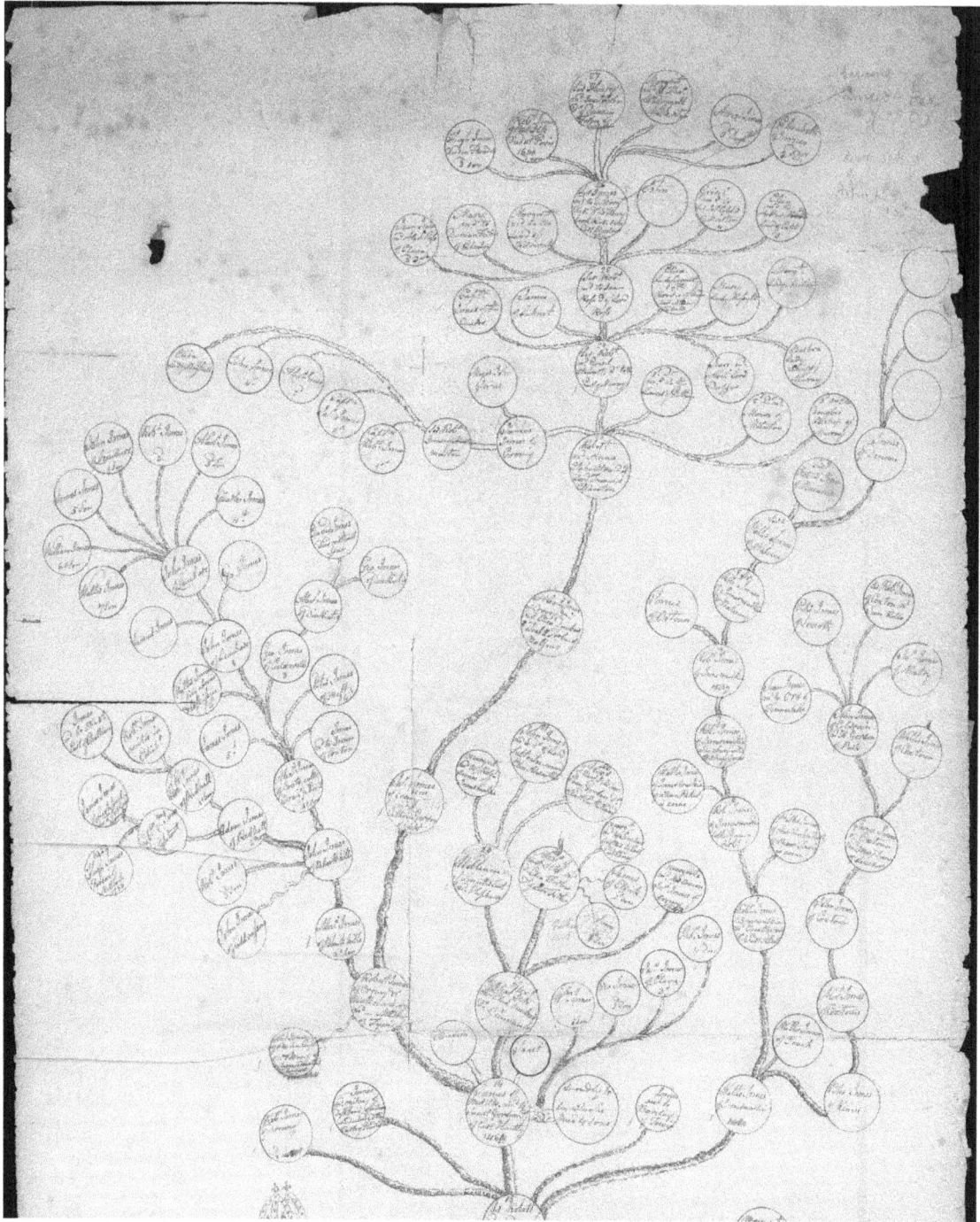

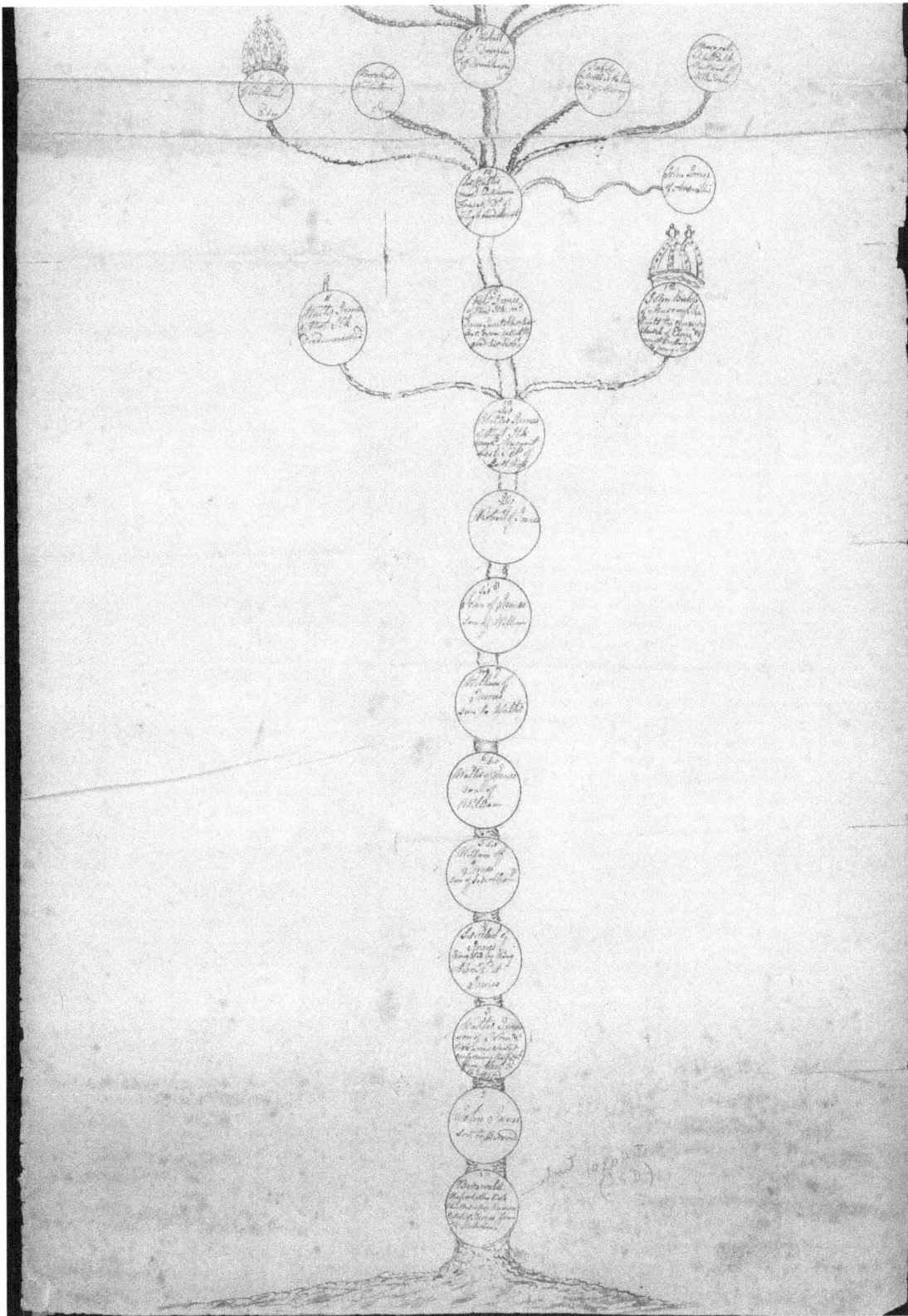

The Innes FamilyTree came from Toney Innes although it appears far older than Toney's generation. Its origin is unknown

# Appendix D: Everett Family Tree

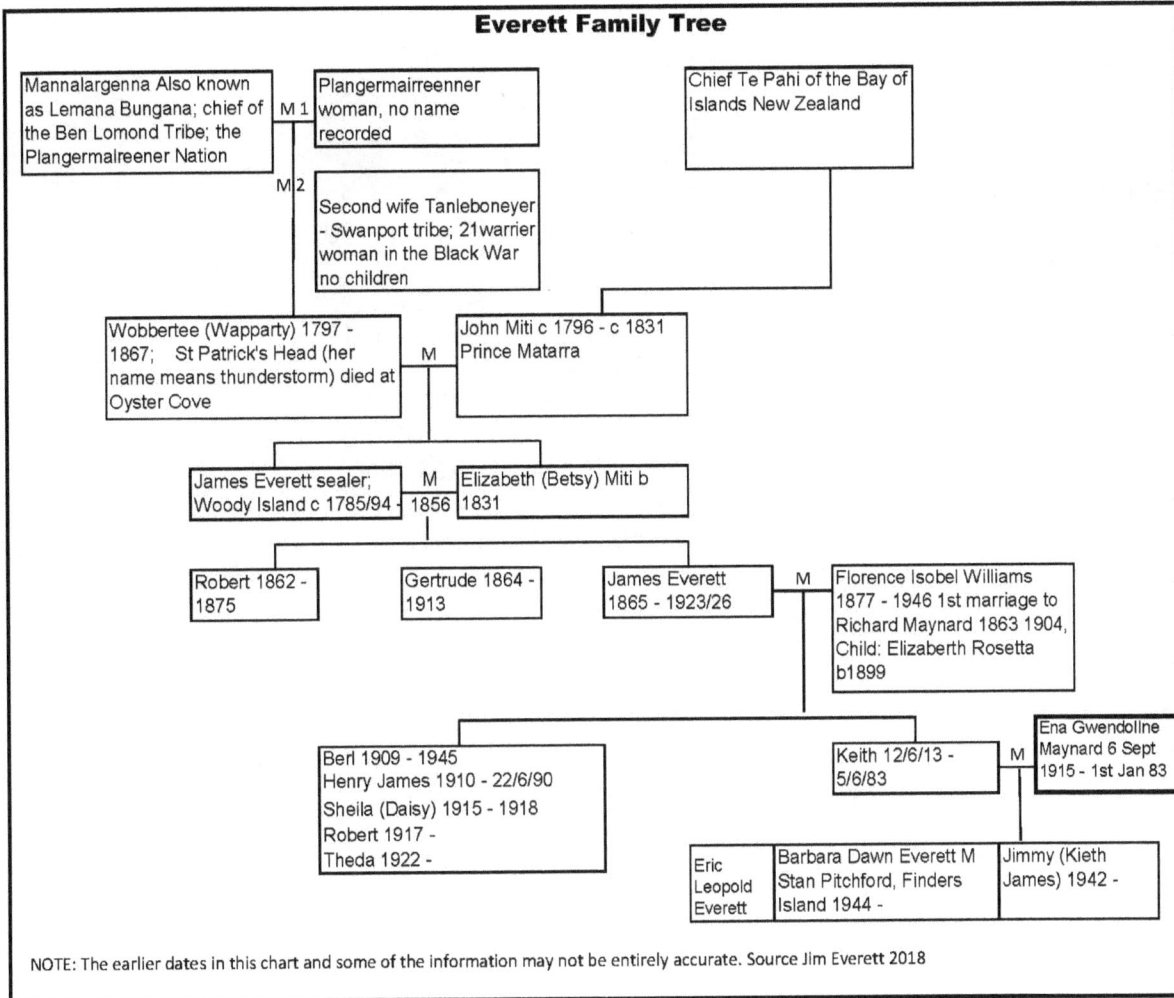

## Everett Family Tree

**Mannalargenna** Also known as Lemana Bungana; chief of the Ben Lomond Tribe; the Plangermalreener Nation

**M 1** — Plangermairreenner woman, no name recorded

**M 2** — Second wife Tanleboneyer - Swanport tribe; 21 warrier woman in the Black War no children

**Chief Te Pahi of the Bay of Islands New Zealand**

**Wobbertee (Wapparty)** 1797 - 1867; St Patrick's Head (her name means thunderstorm) died at Oyster Cove

**M** — **John Miti** c 1796 - c 1831 Prince Matarra

**James Everett** sealer; Woody Island c 1785/94 — **M 1856** — **Elizabeth (Betsy) Miti** b 1831

**Robert** 1862 - 1875

**Gertrude** 1864 - 1913

**James Everett** 1865 - 1923/26 — **M** — **Florence Isobel Williams** 1877 - 1946 1st marriage to Richard Maynard 1863 1904, Child: Elizaberth Rosetta b1899

**Berl** 1909 - 1945
**Henry James** 1910 - 22/6/90
**Sheila (Daisy)** 1915 - 1918
**Robert** 1917 -
**Theda** 1922 -

**Keith** 12/6/13 - 5/6/83 — **M** — **Ena Gwendoline Maynard** 6 Sept 1915 - 1st Jan 83

**Eric Leopold Everett**

**Barbara Dawn Everett** M Stan Pitchford, Finders Island 1944 -

**Jimmy (Kieth James)** 1942 -

NOTE: The earlier dates in this chart and some of the information may not be entirely accurate. Source Jim Everett 2018

NOTES
Chapter Two: Life at Avoca

[ii] Adapted from Tasmanian Archive and Heritage Office Map of the northern located portion of Van Diemen's Land / constructed by J. H. Hughes (Map) [Hobart, Tas./] : [Surveyor-General's Office?], 1837

[iii] Glover, John Richardson. (1850). *Wickford.* http://nla.gov.au/nla.obj-145872955

[iv] Colonial News. (1853, January 29). The Maitland Mercury and Hunter River General Advertiser (NSW 1843 - 1893), p. 4. Retrieved March 10, 2015,

Chapter Five: William Talbot and Catherine

[v] Kingston Rosari 'An overview of the Irish Herbal Tradtion. The Thread that could not be broken sited April 2015

[vi] Malahide, Van Diemen's Land London : Royston & Brown, [n.d.] https://linctas.ent.sirsidynix.net.au/client/en_AU/all/search/results?qu=Malahide&rw=12 sited 26/7/16

Chapter Six: The Fragility of Life

[x] Prout, John Skinner. (1846). *Avoca, V.D.L., Jany 17, '46.* http://nla.gov.au/nla.obj-134406576

[xi] Henrietta's year of birth is confusing. Her marriage certificate in 1848 shows her age at 22 which would place her DOB in 1826. This is at odds with her death notice which in 1899 gives her age as 77 and also her mother would have been in her mid-forties at the time of her birth.

[xii] Thomas Dodd, 'Ross Bridge', undated (ALMFA, SLT) Centre for Tasmanian Historical Studies University of Tasmania http://www.utas.edu.au/library/companion_to_tasmanian_history/A/John%20 Lee%20Archer.htm

Chapter Eight: Frederick Innes and Elizabeth

[xiii] Family Notices (1838, August 7). *Colonial Times (Hobart, Tas. : 1828 - 1857)*, p. 7. Retrieved January 26, 2018, from http://nla.gov.au/nla.news-article8748891

[xiv] SHIP NEWS. (1843, October 17). *Colonial Times (Hobart, Tas. : 1828 - 1857)*, , p. 2. Retrieved August 17, 2016, from http://nla.gov.au/nla.news-article8754109

[xv] *The Silence of Dean Maitland* 1897 Kegan Paul, Trench & Trübner illustrated edition with line drawings by Frederick Hamilton Jackson (1848-1923).

Chapter Ten: Back in V.D.L.

[xvi] THE LATE HON. W. E. NAIRN, MLC (1869, JULY 16) Chronicle (Launceston, Tas: 1835 – 1880) p2

[xvii] *Figure Error! Main Document Only. Family Notices. (1868, May 21. The Mercury (Hobart, Tas. : 1860 - 1954, p. 2. Retrieved March 25, 2015, from http:// nla.gov.au/nla.news-article8852309*

xviii Advertising (1856, January 26). *Colonial Times (Hobart, Tas. : 1828 - 1857)*, , p. 4. Retrieved May 27, 2016, from http://nla.gov.au/nla.news-article8787596

xix *Flying Squadron in the Derwent River, Hobart Town, January 7th, 1870  W. L. Crowther Library, Tasmanian Archive and Heritage Office. In: In: Crowther album (1) Pl. 20 Publisher: Hobart, Tas.: G. Cherry, [1870]*

BOX ONE: EXPEDITION INTO IRELAND, LT COLONEL JOHN GRAY

xx It should be noted that while every effort has been made to verify the information here it should also be acknowledged that there were other John Gray/Greys living during this period. It may that some of the records are not in fact related to the main character of this section which is of course the inherent nature of of any historical  research.

xxi 'House of Lords Journal Volume 7: 28 April 1645', in Journal of the House of Lords: Volume 7, 1644 (London, 1767-1830), pp. 339-341 http://www.british-history.ac.uk/lords-jrnl/vol7/pp339-341 [accessed 6 October 2015].

xxii Nichols, John, *The History and Antiquities of the County of Leister* Vol III Part II, Appendix IV p.30 (Remarkable Passages from Leister' 1642)

xxiii Evans, David Sidney 1995 *The Civil War career of Major-General Edward Massey* (1642- 1647). Kings College London p15

xxiv Groby is pronounced Grooby, like boot and is the current name used for villages owned by the Greys for centuries. The Grey family of Groby was a cadet or junior branch of the big Grey gentry family, which resided in Codnor & Thurrock, Ruthin, Wilton, and Sandiacre & Landford. The horizontal blue and white bands of the Grey shield were varied, as a junior branch of the family, with red discs or roundels. However the Greys of Groby, later, seem to have omitted these roundels.( Alison Coates, Heritage Warden, Groby, Leicestershire November 2015)

xxv Anthony Squires questions the connection with Anchitell Grey pointing out that there is little reliable evidence to support this claim for more than one hundred years after the Doomsday Book in 1088.
Squires Anthony 2002 *The Greys a long and noble line.* The Silk Press Cheshire p9

xxvi Richards J (no date) The Greys of Bradgate in the English Civil War: First Early of Stamford and his Son and Heir Thomas, Lord Grey of Groby p 34

xxvii Ibid p 46

xxviii Calendar of the state papers relating to Ireland preserved in the Public Record Office. 1625-[1670] by Great Britain. Public Record Office; Mahaffy, Robert Pentland, 1871-1943, ed

xxix British Civil Wars, Commonwealth & Protectorate 1638 – 1660;http://bcw- project.org/biography/murrough-obrien-earl-of-inchiquin

xxx Col. Stubbers was amongst those excluded from the terms of the Indemnity and Oblivion Act of 1660, the purpose of which was to grant a general pardon to anyone who had committed crimes during the Civil War and Interregnum, with the exception of certain crimes such as murder. Specifically exempted were those named individuals who had been involved in the regicide of Charles I in 1649. Peter Stubbers was amongst those named as a 'halberdier', i.e. an axeman who had assisted in the execution of the king.
This fact alone, along with his 'swift exit and subsequent disappearance', from Galway following the restoration of Charles I, makes it extremely likely that he had a real case to answer. A document recently discovered in the Bodieian Library , Oxford, by Tr. Jackie Ui Chionna of the History Department at N.U.I Galway, appears to confirm Stubbers involvement in the Execution of Charles 1. The document, written by
King Charles II to the Lords Justices of Ireland from Whitehall on 11 March 1661, states: 'Upon information that a "considerable part of the ancient patrimony" of the King's petitioner Colonel Fitzpatrick, on whose behalf, after reference of his petition to the Marquess of *Ormond & after consideration of the Marquess' report to his Majesty thereupon, the*

*King's letters were lately issued directing his restoration to his estate, - is now "in the possession of one Stubbers, a halberdier, that assisted at that execrable murder of our royal Father... and so exempted by Our "Declaration" from pardon," it is ordered that Fitzpatrick be forthwith restored thereto.'*

Carte Calendar, Volume 31, January - May 1661 (Shelfmark: MS. Carte 42, fol(s). 3 Document type: Original). Bodleian Library, University of Oxford

[xxxi] *Col. Stubbers was amongst those excluded from the terms of the Indemnity and Oblivion Act of 1660, the purpose of which was to grant a general pardon to anyone who had committed crimes during the Civil War and Interregnum, with the exception of certain crimes such as murder. Specifically exempted were those named individuals who had been involved in the regicide of Charles I in 1649. Peter Stubbers was amongst those named as a 'halberdier', i.e. an axeman who had assisted in the execution of the king. This fact alone, along with his 'swift exit and subsequent disappearance', from Galway following the restoration of Charles II, makes it extremely likely that he had a real case to answer. A document recently discovered in the Bodleian Library, Oxford, by Dr. Jackie Uí Chionna of the History Department at N.U.I. Galway, appears to confirm Stubbers involvement in the Execution of Charles 1. The document, written by King Charles II to the Lords Justices of Ireland from Whitehall on 11 March 1661, states: 'Upon information that a "considerable part of the ancient patrimony" of the King's petitioner Colonel Fitzpatrick, on whose behalf, after reference of his petition to the Marquess of Ormond & after consideration of the Marquess' report to his Majesty thereupon, the King's letters were lately issued directing his restoration to his estate, - is now "in the possession of one Stubbers, a halberdier, that assisted at that execrable murder of our royal Father... and so exempted by Our "Declaration" from pardon," it is ordered that Fitzpatrick be forthwith restored thereto.'*
Carte Calendar, Volume 31, January - May 1661
(Shelfmark: MS. Carte 42, fol(s). 3 Document type: Original).
Bodleian Library, University of Oxford

[xxxii] Peter Stubber's Regiment of Foot. *British Civil Wars, Commonwealth & Protectorate 1638 – 1660*; sighted 10/11/15

[xxxiii] Bruce Gaston 2015 Irish History Compressed: A Short History of Ireland Ebook published by Irish History Compressed.

[xxxiv] O'Hart, John 1887 The Irish landed gentry when Cromwell came to Ireland DUBLIN P415

[xxxv] [From the Report of the "Several Proceedings in Parliament," 23rd May to 6th June, 1650.]

[xxxvi] National Library of Ireland GO, MS 530 p142

[xxxvii] Murphy, Denis, 1833-1896 1902 *Cromwell in Ireland, a history of Cromwell's Irish campaign* DUBLIN Gill p17

[xxxviii] THE CROMWELLIAN SETTLEMENT OF IRELAND By JOHN P. PRENDERGAST BARRISTER-AT-LAW IRELAND. THIRD EDITION MELLIFONT PRESS, LTD KILDARE HOUSE, WESTMORELAND STREET, DUBLIN 1922

BOX TWO: LIFE BEYOND THE MILITARY, SPOILS OF WAR

[xxxix] Feehan John 2009 The Landscape of Slieve Bloom – a study of its natural and human heritage. Slieve Bloom Rural Development Society p131

[xl] Murray Paddy 2013 Relating to Roscomroe: a compilation of historical stories, facts and other matters of interest 1305 – 1960's Self published

[xli] Creator: Sanson; Boazio; Speed 1665 Partie meridio.le du royaume d'Irlande Publisher: chez l'autheur From Oldmapsonline.

[xlii] Calendar of the state papers relating to Ireland preserved in the Public Record Office. 1625- [1670] Great Britain. Public Record Office; Mahaffy, Robert Pentland, 1871-1943, ed.

[xliii] O'Hart, John 1887 *The Irish landed gentry when Cromwell came to Ireland* DUBLIN P415

[xliv] Heaney Paddy 2006 At the foot of Slieve Bloom – history and folklore of Cadamstown Kilcormac Historical Society p262

[xlv] Morrison, Ireland Anno 1600 p77 Taken from Feehan John 2009 The Landscape of Slieve Bloom – a study of its natural and human heritage. Slieve Bloom Rural Development Society p107

[xlvi] Journal of the House of Commons: Volume 5, 1646-1648. Originally published by His Majesty's Stationery Office, London, 1802

[xlvii] Deeds and papers of the Basil family of Wilton Park and Drumboe Castle, County Donegal in Ireland and of their heirs the Heyes family, baronets of Drumboe Castle 1620 – 1816 (index D-X 776/8)

[xlviii] Ball, F. Elrington The Judges in Ireland, 1221-1921 John Murray London 1926 p383

[xlix] Hawkes, Richard 2015 direct descendent from William Caulfeild, 1st Viscount Charlemont Mary Caulfeild's brother.

[l] Ball, F. Erlington 1902 (Francis Elrington), d. 1928 A history of the County Dublin; the people, parishes and antiquities from the earliest times to the close of the eighteenth century. Dublin p 165

[li] D'Alton, John, 1792-1867 1845 The History of Ireland Dublin, Published by the Author p61

[lii] Richard Hawkes (1/12/15 an eminent Caulfeild expert and family researcher questions whether Fermanagh is infact correct. "I have Aidan Clarke's excellent 'Prelude to Restoration in Ireland'. I hesitate to suggest this to such an informed writer but I think the reference to Fermanagh is an error, possibly intending Armagh. Sir William spent the latter part of his life as the resident governor of Fort Charlemont on the Blackwater River in County Armagh, and I think it is likely that Mary and most of his children were born either there or at Boyle Abbey, but we have no evidence."

[liii] Aidan Clark 2004 Prelude to Restoration in Ireland: The End of the Commonwealth, 1659– 1660 Cambridge University Press p42

[liv/liv] Stirnet Limited Abbey View Riverdale Abbeydore Herefordshire HR2 0AJ United Kingdom [lv/lv] Hawkes, Richard 2015 direct descendent from William Caulfeild, 1st Viscount Charlemont Mary Caulfeild's brother

BOX THREE: ROSCOMROE AND THE GREY MANSION

[lvi] Depositions of 1641, Trinity College Dublin. [vii] Annals of the Dioceses of Killaloe

[lviii] Depositions, 1641, Trinity College Dublin [lix] Census of the Barony of Ballybritt, 1659 [lx] Register of deeds, Ireland
BOX FOUR: REASONS TO EMIGRATE

[lxi] Heaney Paddy 2006 'At the Foot of Slieve Bloom. History of Folklore of Cadamstown'
Kilcormac Historical Society p266

[lxii] Further reading on this topic; Heaney Paddy 2006 ibid
Murray Paddy 2013 'Relating to Roscomroe' p55 Self Published
Feehan John 2009 'The landscape of Slieve Bloom' Slieve Bloom Rural Development Society

[lxiii] PRIMARY EDUCATION. (1886, My 7). Lauceston Examiner (Tas. 1842-1899), p4 Retrieved 31 July 2015 from http://nla.gov.au/nla.news-article36697474

[lxiv] Feehan John 2009 'The landscape of Slieve Bloom' Slieve Bloom Rural Development Society p133

[lxv] Dougharty K H 1953 A Story of a Pioneering Family in Van Diemen's Land Self Published

[lxvi] Connaught Journal Galway, Ireland, Monday, March 3, 1823 Volume 69 Price 5 Pence

BOX FIVE: INDIVIDUAL REASONS FOR LEAVING

[lxvii] War Office 5th Feb 1824 *A list of the officers and Army and Royal Marines on full, retired and half pay*

lxviii Bloom, H. (2010). *Jane Austen's Emma.* Infobase    Publishing

lxix Major William Gray and the late Staff Surgeon Dochard *Travels in Western Africa in the years 1818,19,20 and 21 from the River Gambia, through Woolli, Bondoo, Galam Kasson, Kaarta and Foolidoo to the River Niger* by with a map, drawings, and costumes, illustrative of those countries London: John Murray, Albemarle Street MDCCCXXV (1825) Preface

lxx For more information on Major Gray as magistrate refer to Dillon Margaret *'Convict Labour and Colonial Society in the Campbell Town Police District: 1820-1839'*,

lxxi Dougharty K H 1953 *A Story of a Pioneering Family in Van Diemen's Land* Self Published p8 This may not be a factual description of events as they really occurred but these can be researched easily. Major William Gray's book on his expedition is now available online

lxxii Major William Gray and the late Staff Surgeon Dochard  op cit p163-64

lxxiii Major William Gray and the late Staff Surgeon Dochard ibid

lxxiv Dane Kennedy *Forgotten Failures of African Exploration* The Public Domain Review https://publicdomainre-view.org/2015/04/22/forgotten-failures-of-african-exploration/ sited Feb 9th 2018

lxxv Image of ceremonial attire featured in *Travels in Western Africa in the Years 1818, 19, 20, and 21 from the River Gambia, through Woolli, Gondoo, Galam, Kasson, Kaarta, and Foolidoo, to the River Niger*

lxxvi FINANCE ACCOUNTS OF THE UNITED KINGDOM, IN EIGHT CLASSES, FOR THE YEAR 1828 p300

lxxviilxxvii Dougharty K H 1953 *op cit* p6

## BOX SIX: JOURNEY TO VDL, THE GREY FAMILY

lxxviii *Hibernian Magazine* 1812 p189

lxxix Henrietta's year of birth is confusing. Her marriage certificate in 1848 shows her age at 22 which would place her DOB in 1826. This is at odds with her death notice which in 1899 gives her age as 77 and also her mother would have been in her mid-forties at the time of her birth.

lxxx Murray Frank My Early Pioneers and Their Families Website

lxxxi Dublin Freeman's Journal 19.12.1828; London Times 29.12.1828. courtesy of Frank Murray

lxxxii Humphrey came ashore with 1000 sovereigns his money belt intact which provided the family with sufficient funds to continue with their journey and life in VDL

lxxxiii Murray Frank My Early Pioneers and Their Families Website

lxxxiv In fact the journey took slightly under one year, 20 July 1828 – 3rd June 1829. The Marine Department Arrival Record MB2/39/1 page 13 is incorrectly headed 1830 (Frank Murray)

lxxxv THE HOBART-TOWN COURIER. (1829, June 13). *The Hobart Town Courier (Tas. : 1827 - 1839)*, p. 2. Retrieved January 30, 2018, from http://nla.gov.au/nla.news- article4216056

lxxxvi COLONIAL TIMES (1829, June 12).*Colonial Times (Hobart, Tas. : 1828 - 1857)*, , p. 3. Retrieved June 22, 2016, from http://nla.gov.au/nla.news-article8644313

lxxxvii Tasmanian Archive and Heritage Office Map of the northern located portion of Van Diemen's Land / constructed by J. H. Hughes (Map) [Hobart, Tas./] : [Surveyor-General's Office?], 1837

## BOX SEVEN: JOURNEY TO AVOCA, THE GRAY FAMILY

lxxxviii SHIPPING & COMMERCIAL INTELLIGENCE, ARRIVED AT HOBART-TOWM, (1827, August 25).*Hobart Town Gazette (Tas. : 1825 - 1827)*, , p. 5. Retrieved May 19, 2016, from http://nla.gov.au/nla.news-article8790896

lxxxix Newitt, L., & Jones, A. (1988). Convicts and carriageways: Tasmanian road development until 1880.

xc Department of State Growth, Tasmanian Government. St Pauls River Bridge Replacement Development Application Supporting Report May 2015

xci Ellen was the daughter of James Kingsley (1756-1816) and Ismenia Bell, they were married in 1792, Killahoe diocese. This was his second marriage. First married to Ursula Melsop, married in 1779. James and Ismenia had the following children: Jimenia 1793-1801, James Bell , Samuel Bell 1801-1865 married Dorothea Maunsell also came to VDL. William 1804-1887. Charles, Mary Annabelle, Ellen,  Diana Jane Bell 1800-1887 xcii Dougharty Kate 1953 *The Story of a Pioneering Family in Van Diemen's Land* self-published p9

xciii Lt James Gray b 1795 d 18th May 1849; Mary Gray (nee Legge) b 1802 d 9th Oct 1865

xciv Frances married Captain Alfred Darby and died on the 5th July 1873 at Rushwood Victoria.

Family Notices (1873, July 16). *The Mercury (Hobart, Tas. : 1860 - 1954)*, , p. 1. Retrieved May 24, 2016, from http://nla.gov.au/nla.news-article8927033

xcv Blanche Eliza never married and lived to 85. She died at St Kilda, Victoria 12 August 1911

xcvi Robert Legge was granted land and settled at Cullenswood on the eastern end of the Fingal Valley on the banks of the Break O' Day River.

xcvii Information curtesy of Jenny Stiles. Web site entitled *Legge Family of Rodeen & Garrane [Garvane], Tipperary, Limerick, Dublin & Tasmania.*

xcviii Family influence with R. W. Hay at the Colonial Office led to his appointment as first assistant surveyor of Van Diemen's Land in 1826 and he arrived in the colony in July 1827. http://adb.anu.edu.au/biography/frankland-george-2064

xcix lxv Newitt, L., & Jones, A. (1988). Convicts and carriageways: Tasmanian road development until 1880. P44

c CHRONOLOGY OF 1827, FOR VAN DIEMEN'S LAND. (1827, December 29). *The Hobart Town Courier (Tas. : 1827 - 1839)*, , p. 4. Retrieved June 6, 2016, from http://nla.gov.au/nla.news- article4225132

ci CHRONOLOGY OF 1827, FOR VAN DIEMEN'S LAND. (1827, December 29). *The Hobart Town Courier (Tas. : 1827 - 1839)*, , p. 4. Retrieved June 6, 2016, from http://nla.gov.au/nla.news- article4225132

cii Archives of Tasmania https://stors.tas.gov.au/RGD32-1-1-p197j2k sited 14/02/2018

ciii This journey and many others in Tasmania is cleverly described in Newitt, L., & Jones, A. (1988). Convicts and carriageways: Tasmanian road development until 1880.

civ Newitt, L., & Jones, A. (1988). Convicts and carriageways: Tasmanian road development until 1880 . P76

cv Prinsep, M. A. (Ed.). (1833). *The journal of a voyage from Calcutta to Van Diemen's Land: comprising a description of that colony during a six months' residence.* Smith, Elder, and Company. P81-82

cvi Meredith, M. C. (1852). *My Home in Tasmania, during a residence of nine years* (Vol. 1). P53


BOX SEVEN: HOUSES AS A REFLECTION OF CHARACTER

cvii There remains some confusion in relation to James' rank whether it was Lieutenant or Captain. The ship records on arrival state Lieut. Gray (Colonial Times and Tasmanian Advertiser 24th August 1827 as well in his wife's death notice but the traveller of 1833 refers to him as Captain as well as BURKE'S COLONIAL GENTRY. 1891 p357)

cviii Dougharty Kate op cit p8

cix Col. George Arthur (1784-1854) was Governor of VDL from May 1824 to Oct 1836

cx Franklin was appointed Lieutenant-Governor of Van Diemen's Land in 1836, but was removed from office in 1843.

cxi Dougharty Kate op cit p33

cxii Port Phillip Gazette Wed 1 May 1839

cxiii Hobart Town Gazette and Southern Reporter (Tas. : 1816 - 1821), Saturday 23 January 1819, page 2

cxiv Dillon Margaret C *Convict Labour and Colonial Society in the Campbell Town Police District: 1820-1839.* Degree of Doctor of Philosophy (Ph. D.) University of Tasmania April 2008 p56

cxv Dillon  Margaret C ibid p56

cxvi Dillon   Margaret C ibid p56

cxvii *The Hobart Town Courier*, Saturday 16 October 1830, p.2

cxviii Everett Jim unpublished

cxix Ryan, L. (2012). *Tasmanian Aborigines: a  history since 1803.* Allen   & Unwin.p116

cxx Arthur declared Martial Law on November 1st 1826 and lasted for three years the longest in Australian History (Ryan p105)

cxxi Ryan notes that some Tasmanian Aborigines called Tasmania Trouwanna. P6

cxxii (*N.T.B. Plomley The Tasmanian Tribes and Cicatrices as tribal indicators among the Tasmanian Aborigines.* Queen  Victoria Museum  and  Art  Gallery Date unknown)

cxxiii Ryan, L. (2012). Op cit  p11

cxxiv xc Ryan, L. (2012). Op cit  p29.

cxxv *Telling Places in Country (TPIC)* Historical Biographies University of Tasmania Jan 2015

cxxvi Moulteheerlargenna or Eumarrah was a powerful leader at the time and is well worth studying further. Material is readily   available.

cxxvii Ryan, L. (2012). Op cit  p11

cxxviii Ryan, L. (2012). Op cit  p29

cxxix McMahon John F *THE BRITISH ARMY AND THE COUNTER-INSURGENCY CAMPAIGN IN VAN DIEMEN'S LAND WITH PARTICULAR REFERENCE TO THE BLACK LINE* Submitted in fulfilment of the requirements for the degree of Master of Humanities, University of Tasmania, December 1995 Johnson, M., & McFarlane, I. (2015). *Van Diemen's Land: An Aboriginal History.* UNSW Press. *Colonial Secretary's Office, September 25, 1830.* Source: *Hobart Town Gazette,* GOVERNMENT ORDER. Notice 6 [1830] No. 11.Colonial Secretary's Office
BOX TEN: WAR AND SURVIVAL 1829 -  32

cxxx Dougharty K H 1953 op cit p33

cxxxi No title (1828, August 1). *The Australian (Sydney, NSW : 1824 - 1848),* , p. 2. Retrieved May 20, 2016, from http://nla.gov.au/nla.news-article36865685

cxxxii 1829, February 9). *Launceston Advertiser (Tas. : 1829 - 1846),* , p. 2. Retrieved June 16, 2016, from http://nla.gov.au/nla.news-page8721080

cxxxiii IMPROMPTU (1829, April 13). *Launceston Advertiser (Tas. : 1829 - 1846),* , p. 3. Retrieved June 16, 2016, from http://nla.gov.au/nla.news-article84776091

cxxxiv Bonwick, J. (1884). *The lost Tasmanian race.* S. Low, Marston, Searle, and Rivington p118

cxxxv Bonwick, J. (1884). ibid. p62

cxxxvi Commonwealth Government of Australia. 12 June 1986. *Recognition of Aboriginal Customary Laws (ALRC Report 31) sec 65*

cxxxvii *Travels in Western Africa in the years 1818,19,20 and 21 from the River Gambia, through Woolli, Bondoo, Galam Kasson, Kaarta and Foolidoo to the River Niger* by Major William Gray and the      late Staff Surgeon Dochard with a map, drawings, and costumes, illustrative of those countries London: John Murray, Albemarle Street MDCCCXXV (1825) Preface

cxxxviii Australian Government Australian Law Reform Commission. (ALRC Report 31) 12 June 1986 Recognition of Aboriginal Customary Laws at Common Law: The Settled Colony Debate

cxxxix Website 'Sri Lanka's forest-dwellers the Veddas or Wanniyalaeto

cxl Transcribed by Lynne Palmer, Peter Mayo, Donna Gallacher, John Brooker http://acms.sl.nsw.gov.au/_transcript/2007/D00007/a1771.html

cxli Bonwick, J. (1870). *The Last of the Tasmanians: Or, The Black War of Van Diemen's Land: With Numerous Illustrations and Coloured Engravings.* Sampson Low, Son & Marston. Chapter 6 cxlii cx [No heading]. (1829, February 9). *Launceston Advertiser* (Tas. : 1829 - 1846), p. 2. Retrieved July 13, 2015, from http://nla.gov.au/nla.news-page8721080

cxliii Assumed to be Major William although unstated.

cxliv Desailly, B. (1977). *The mechanics of genocide colonial policies and attitudes towards the Tasmanian Aborigines, 1824-1836* (Doctoral dissertation, University of Tasmania). P47

cxlv Desailly, B. (1977) ibid P142

cxlvi [*Colonial Times*, 1 October 1830, p. 3.]

cxlvii Desailly, B. (1977). Op cit P143

cxlviii McMahon, John. *"The Black Line: Military Operations in Van Diemen's Land,* October To November 1830". *Tasmanian Historical Research Association Papers & Proceedings.* Volume 55 Part 3 [December] 2008 pp.175-182 [including diagrams]; originally presented on 2 November 2007 at the biennial conference of the Tasmanian Historical Societies at Richmond. The conference theme was 'Defending the Colony: the military in Tasmania'. P 44

cxlix McMahon, John. *"The Black Line: Military Operations in Van Diemen's Land,* October To November 1830". *Tasmanian Historical Research Association Papers & Proceedings.* Volume 55 Part 3 [December] 2008 pp.175-182 [including diagrams]; originally presented on 2 November 2007 at the biennial conference of the Tasmanian Historical Societies at Richmond. The conference theme was 'Defending the Colony: the military in Tasmania'. P 44

cl *levy en masse* is 'the conscription of the civilian population in large numbers in the face of impending invasion. *Also called*: levée en masse(*French* ləve ã mas)' Collins Online Dictionary
sited 20/6/16

cli *Black War ~ Van Diemen's Land* CSO 7578 GOVERNMENT ORDER. Notice 6 [1830] No. 11. Colonial Secretary's Office.

clii *The Hobart Town Courier*, Saturday 25 September 1830, p.2 cliii *The Hobart Town Courier*, Saturday 16 October 1830, p.2 cliv Austen Jane *Emma* p157

clv Dougharty K H 1953 *op cit* p53

clvi Annual report by Aborigines Protection Society (Great Britain); Aborigines Protection Society (Great Britain). Pamphlets Published 1838

BOX ELEVEN: A NEW WAY OF LIFE BEGINS

clvii Dove, H.S. (1924) . Some Rare Birds in Tasmania. *Emu* 24 , 280–282

clviii Advertising (1837, March 30). *Launceston Advertiser (Tas. : 1829 - 1846)*, p. 1. Retrieved January 26, 2018, from http://nla.gov.au/nla.news-article84752780

clix THE GAZETTE. (1840, August 7). *The Hobart Town Courier and Van Diemen's Land Gazette (Tas. : 1839 - 1840)*, , p. 2. Retrieved May 26, 2016, from http://nla.gov.au/nla.news- article8747975

clx Advertising (1836, May 5). *Launceston Advertiser (Tas. : 1829 - 1846)*, p. 1. Retrieved January 24, 2018, from http://nla.gov.au/nla.news-article84753553

clxi The Courier. (1834, June 13). *The Hobart Town Courier (Tas. : 1827 - 1839)*, p. 2. Retrieved February 1, 2018, from http://nla.gov.au/nla.news-article4184725

clxii Classified Advertising. (1835, July 17). *The Hobart Town Courier* (Tas. : 1827 - 1839), p. 4. Retrieved October 3, 2015, from http://nla.gov.au/nla.news-article4179766

clxiii C:\Users\Owner\Documents\Dougharty\Bush Rangers\The Sydney Herald (NSW 1831 - 1842), Thursday 1 September 1836, page 2 a_files

clxiv PROCEEDINGS (1844, April 24). *The Cornwall Chronicle (Launceston, Tas. : 1835 - 1880)*, p. 2. Retrieved February 1, 2018, from http://nla.gov.au/nla.news-article66019880

clxv No Title (1858, January 9). *Launceston Examiner (Tas. : 1842 - 1899)*, p. 2

(AFTERNOON). Retrieved February 1, 2018, from http://nla.gov.au/nla.news- article38990270

BOX THIRTEEN: CONVICTS AND THE GRAY FAMILIES

clxvi The common, lower classes; the hoi polloi. This rather disparaging term was coined by the Victorian novelist and playwright Edward Bulwer-Lytton. He used it in his 1830 novel Paul Clifford The

Phrase Finder.

clxvii Archives of Tasmania NAME_INDEXES: 1375398 clxviii Archives of Tasmania NAME_INDEXES 1375396 clxix Archives of Tasmania NAME_INDEXES: 1375387 clxx Archives of Tasmania NAME_INDEXES: 1390691

clxxi Cowley, T. M., & Snowden, D. M. (2013). Patchwork Prisoners. The Rajah Quilt and the women who made it.

clxxii Archives of Tasmania NAME_INDEXES: 1394810

clxxiii POLICE OFFICE.—THIS DAY. (1859, January 13). The Courier (Hobart, Tas. : 1840 - 1859), , p. 3. Archives Office of Tasmania – digitised record Item: CON40-1-7

clxxiv Archives Office of Tasmania NAME_INDEXES:1428131 clxxv Archives Office of Tasmania NAME_INDEXES:1438208 clxxvi Archives Office of Tasmania NAME_INDEXES:1410230 clxxvii Hobart Town Courier Friday June 1834 page 2

clxxviii AVOCA CENTENARIAN. (1932, February 12). The Mercury(Hobart, Tas. : 1860 - 1954), p. 2.

NOTE: Miss J Grey was probably Frances Ann Talbot Gray, b 1833 clxxix Archives Office of Tasmania NAME_INDEXES:1178141 clxxx Archives Office of Tasmania NAME_INDEXES: 143954

clxxxi Assignments. (1838, June 1). The Hobart Town Courier (Tas. : 1827 - 1839), , p. 1. Retrieved March 2, 2016, from http://nla.gov.au/nla.news-article4164706

clxxxii Advertising (1839, March 30). The Cornwall Chronicle (Launceston, Tas. : 1835 - 1880), , p. 3. Retrieved March 2, 2016, from http://nla.gov.au/nla.news-article65949717

clxxxiii Advertising (1839, March 30). The Cornwall Chronicle (Launceston, Tas. : 1835 - 1880), , p. 3. Retrieved March 2, 2016, from http://nla.gov.au/nla.news-article65949717

BOX FOURTEEN: WILLIAM TALBOT, A RING AND CATHERINE

clxxxiv Neapolitan Fever is brucellosis
1. An infectious disease in humans caused by some species of bacteria of the genus Brucell
a, that is transmitted by contact with infected animals or raw milk products and marked by fever,

malaise, severe headache, and jointpain. Also called *Gibraltar fever*, *Malta fever*, *Mediterranean fever*, *undulant fever*. (and Neapolitan fever)
(Farlex *The Free Dictionary* – sighted 12 August 15)

clxxxv Claddagh Ring Website http://www.claddaghring.com/How-to-wear-claddagh-rings- a/122.htm

clxxxvi Murphy, Colin, and Donal O'Dea (2006) The Feckin' Book of Everything Irish. New York, Barnes & Noble. p.126 ISBN 0-7607-8219-9

clxxxvii British Museum http://www.britishmuseum.org/research/collection_online/collection_object_details.aspx?obje ctId=79510&partId=1&people=93030&peoA=93030-3-5&page=1

clxxxviii James, S. E. (2016). *Women's Voices in Tudor Wills, 1485–1603: Authority, Influence and Material Culture.* Routledge. P82

clxxxix Luminarium Encyclopedia Project. England under the Tudors sited March 2015

cxc Luminarium Encyclopedia Project. England under the Tudors sited March 2015

cxci Robert Stedall Mary Queen of Scotts.net http://www.maryqueenofscots.net/people/bess- hardwick-countess- shrewsbury/ sighted 28/7/16

cxcii Family Notices (1902, April 1). *The Mercury (Hobart, Tas. : 1860 - 1954),* , p. 1. Retrieved July 21, 2016, from http://nla.gov.au/nla.news-article9580553

cxciii No title (1902, April 1). *Daily Telegraph (Launceston, Tas. : 1883 - 1928)*, p. 2. Retrieved February 2, 2018, from http://nla.gov.au/nla.news-article153798474

BOX FIFTEEN: BUILDING A CHURCH
cxciv Backhouse, James. (2013). pp. 152-3. *The Life and Labours of George Washington Walker, of Hobart Town, Tasmania.* London: Forgotten Books. (Original work published 1862)

cxcv Port Phillip Gazette Saturday April 27 1839

cxcvi QVM:1987:P:0827. View of Avoca, Tasmania, 1855, from a drawing by Emily Bowring.

cxcvii DOING THE AMIABLE. (1842, May 28). *Launceston Examiner (Tas. : 1842 - 1899)*, , p. 4 (EVENING). RetrievedAugust10,2016,fromhttp://nla.gov.au/nla.news-article36248666

cxcviii THE PETITION OF THE CLERGY (1845, August 6). *The Courier (Hobart, Tas. : 1840 - 1859)*, , p. 4. Retrieved June 9, 2016, from http://nla.gov.au/nla.news-article2947765

cxcix Prinsep, M. A. (Ed.). (1833). *The journal of a voyage from Calcutta to Van Diemen's Land: comprising a description of that colony during a six months' residence.* Smith, Elder, and Company. P89

cc It should be noted that Ellinthorpe is also spelt Ellinthorp. The former may have referred to the school and the latter to the property. (See Stilwell article)

cci Stilwell G.T. Mr and Mrs. George Carr Clark of "Ellinthorp Hall" A paper read before a General Meeting of The Association on 15th September 1962 p80

ccii Stilwell G.T Ibid p86

cciii Stilwell G.T. Ibid p86

BOX SEVENTEEN: CHANGING TIMES 1840 – 1849

BOX EIGHTEEN: DEATH OF WILLIAM AND JAMES
cciv Family Notices (1848, March 18). *The Courier (Hobart, Tas. : 1840 - 1859)*, p. 2. Retrieved February 2, 2018, from http://nla.gov.au/nla.news-article2969610

ccv Family Notices (1853, March 22). *Launceston Examiner (Tas. : 1842 - 1899)*, , p. 3 (AFTERNOON). Retrieved August 16, 2016, from http://nla.gov.au/nla.news-article36268550 ccvi Family Notices (1869, December 31). *The Argus (Melbourne, Vic. : 1848 - 1957)*, , p. 4. Retrieved May 19, 2016, from http://nla.gov.au/nla.news-article5809458

ccvii Tasmania. Land Commissioners. (1962). *Journals of the Land Commissioners for Van Diemen's Land, 1826-28.* A. McKay (Ed.). University of Tasmania, in conjunction with the

Tasmanian Historical Research Association p90.

ccviiiccviii Dickens C 1850 David Copperfield ch 12

ccix GENERAL POST OFFICE. (1841, September 3). *The Courier (Hobart, Tas. : 1840 - 1859)*, ,
p. 4. Retrieved May 19, 2016, from http://nla.gov.au/nla.news-article2955699 and research conducted by Jerry Weirich

ccx Advertising (1847, December 11).*Launceston Examiner (Tas. : 1842 - 1899)*, , p. 7 (AFTERNOON). Retrieved
May 25, 2016, from http://nla.gov.au/nla.news-article36253593 ccxi Family Notices (1853, December 6).*Launceston Examiner (Tas. : 1842 - 1899)*, , p. 2 (AFTERNOON). Retrieved May 24, 2016, from http://nla.gov.au/nla.news-article36270707

ccxii Family Notices (1865, October 21). *The Cornwall Chronicle (Launceston, Tas. : 1835 - 1880)*,
, p. 8. Retrieved May 24, 2016, from http://nla.gov.au/nla.news-article72360680

ccxiii x *The Cruise of The Flying Squadron 1869 – 1870* by Marcus McCausland. This is a diary of an Ensign who was
on the voyage. Charles Fountain May 2002

ccxiv Davis Peter. Zeist, The Netherlands *William Loney RN – Life and Career* Website

ccxv *The Cruise of The Flying Squadron 1869 – 1870* by Marcus McCausland. This is a diary of an Ensign who was
on the voyage. Charles Fountain May 2002

ccxvi Flying Squadron, 1869-1870 *under the command of Rear-Admiral G.T. Phipps Hornby*
[compiled by J.B. and Henry Cavendish].Published 1871 p156

ccxvii THE CRUISE OF THE FLYING SQUADRON. (1871, September 26). *The Mercury* (Hobart, Tas. : 1860 - 1954),
p. 3. Retrieved March 4, 2015, from http://nla.gov.au/nla.news-article8873497 ccxviii Flying Squadron, 1869-1870 *under the
command of Rear-Admiral G.T. Phipps Hornby* [compiled by J.B. and Henry Cavendish].Published 1871 p156

Appendix B
ccxix Apparently there is a direct link between these willows and the ones at Plenty in the Derwent Valley in Tasmania
HISTORIC TREES. (1939, July 25). *The Mercury* (Hobart, Tas. : 1860 - 1954), p. 10. Retrieved September 4, 2015, from
http://nla.gov.au/nla.news-article25596626
As well as many other places in Australia and around the World

www.ingramcontent.com/pod-product-compliance
Lightning Source LLC
Chambersburg PA
CBHW081231090426
42738CB00016B/3260